NARRACION HISTORICA

Don Pio Pico, 1801-1894
From a photograph of 1858.
Courtesy of the Bancroft Library, Berkeley, California.

Don Pio Pico's
Historical Narrative

translated by the late
Arthur P. Botello

edited with introduction by
Martin Cole and Henry Welcome

THE ARTHUR H. CLARK COMPANY
Glendale, California   1973

Dedicated to the memory of

ARTHUR BOTELLO

whose translation made possible this volume

Contents

Foreword

The visitor, driving in and around Los Angeles and seeing the name Pico perpetuated, may pause and wonder about the man. Indeed Don Pío Pico is remembered by the major Pico Boulevard, a city bearing his name with its Pico School and Pico Park, the Pío Pico State Historical Monument with its Pico Mansion, the landmark Pico House in old Los Angeles, by Pico Canyon north of the city, and Pico Creek near Oceanside. His name is commercialized – scores of "Pico" businesses are listed in California directories. And yet, despite the veneration, Pico, the real man is little known. For more than many another *Californio,* he is best remembered by colorful legends supporting his memory.

According to the legend-makers, Pío Pico lived an adventurous storybook life, and in a large sense this is true. It seems rather strange that the writers of legends should deviate from truth, when on examining documents, the elements of romance and adventure almost exceed some of the wildest stories that have persisted in books, magazines and newspapers.

In his early manhood Pío Pico was first and foremost a revolutionist. It is necessary to understand that revolutions and counter-revolutions in the Mexican period were the accepted manner for political advancement.

Governorships during those years of unrest sometimes changed several times a year, and a governor might be in and out and then back in office in a short space of time. One persistent protagonist was Pío Pico.

In 1831 Pico was leading his first revolution. It was against Governor Victoria. Governor Victoria led an army down from Monterey to crush the young rebel chief, and although Pico did not fight with his rebels, they were sufficiently inspired to rout Victoria's army.

This victory paved the way for Pico's first governorship, but as the terms of governorships could be reckoned in months rather than years, it is not surprising that Pico was relieved of office after several months. Quite understandably, the successful revolution, together with the governorship, put Pico well on the road to influence. For the next decade he was to make the most of it.

The secularization of the missions gave him opportunities to gain financial wealth, as well as the 133,400-acre Rancho Santa Margarita y Las Flores. Now having experience at fomenting revolutions, Pico attempted to oust Governor Alvarado in 1838. It did not quite come off. Instead Pico was captured and returned a prisoner to Santa Barbara, but so great was his influence that he was immediately released.

The political conflict between the rebel and the Monterey governors continued until 1845, when he again revolted. Governor Micheltorena marched an army against Pico's rebels at Los Angeles. A victory for Pico's forces at the Battle of Cahuenga Pass established Pico for the second time in the governor's chair. Now there was more than internal affairs to reckon with. The storm clouds of a gringo war were hovering on the horizon.

The following year the governor's rule was interrupted by the American invasion. Pico, unable to fight the war without adequate finances, escaped to Mexico to seek aid. But his manner of escaping from the Americans was not in the manner the legend-makers would have us believe. The legend-makers down-graded the real story. Instead of an old-fashioned melodrama, they should have told what actually happened, as Pico's experience does have elements of suspense and danger. Mexico's neglect to give aid to Pico eased the way for Kearny, Stockton and Fremont to conquer California in 1846-47.

Pico's life is divided into two parts – the Mexican and the American. It is in the American period that we see a paradoxical change in the man Pico. In the Mexican period he is first a revolutionist, and second an opportunist. In the American period he catches the spirit that is so manifestly American. He is for progress and order. He uses his wealth and influence to establish education, banking, and town development. Among his public endeavors, he serves as a Los Angeles councilman, builds the magnificent Pico House on Main Street, and pioneers in California's first oil venture that eventually grows to become the Standard Oil Company of California. He also increased his land holdings, including the Rancho Paso de Bartolo, where he built a ranch house that has come to be known as the Pico Mansion. Ironically, it was on this ranch that the last California battle of the Mexican War was fought, and the defeat of the Mexicans here brought about the final surrender to the Americans.

As the years crept by, the widowed Pío Pico retired more and more to his ranch home on the banks of the San Gabriel River. Here he watched a new world passing his door-step. The town of Whittier was abuilding on a nearby hillside. All the signs indicated the beloved pastoral era was closing. Newcomers were jostling Mexicans and Americans alike for places in the warm and fruitful sun. They would jostle Pío Pico out of vast wealth and leave him destitute.

The pitiful example of Pío Pico's downfall is more or less typical of how the land-owning Dons were reduced in wealth. Their old-world simplicity and trustfulness of character, and their unstinted hospitality and carelessness in monetary affairs, made them easy prey for unscrupulous adventurers.

In 1883 Pío Pico borrowed $62,000 from one Bernard Cohn. There had been previous business deals with Cohn, and Pío Pico trusted him. At the time of the transaction Pío Pico was over eighty years of age, unable to speak or understand English, but more than that he was utterly bewildered by the complicated ways of American affairs. He was in temporary financial stress, and in his trusting way he turned to Cohn. In the conduct of negotiations Pico relied upon an interpreter, one Pancho Johnson of Mexican-Irish ancestry. Pancho Johnson has been described by Eugene Plummer as having "swindled many an old Don."

To obtain the loan Pico surrendered a deed to all his properties, principally Rancho Paso de Bartolo, with an understanding the document was supporting a mort-

gage, and not a conveyance of title. The estimated value
of the property was $200,000.

Two months later Pico tendered $65,000 to discharge
this debt. Cohn refused settlement on the grounds he
had purchased the property outright. Pico brought suit,
and to his amazement heard Pancho Johnson on the
witness stand testify that the transaction was an unqual-
ified conveyance and not a mortgage.

Pico *vs*. Cohn moved through the courts, and seven
years later the property had doubled in value when the
case terminated in the California Supreme Court. The
court's review, and shameful decision, was, in part:

> . . . And we think it is settled beyond controversy that a
> decree will not be vacated merely because it was obtained by
> forged documents or perjured testimony. The reason for this rule
> is, that there must be an end of litigation   . . .
> . . . Endless litigation, in which nothing was ever finally de-
> termined, would be worse than occasional miscarriages of justice;
> and so the rule is, that a final judgment cannot be annulled
> merely because it can be shown to have been based on perjured
> testimony; for if this could be done once, it would be done again
> and again *ad infinitum*.   . .

The end came for Pío Pico on September 11, 1894,
at the home of his daughter, Joaquina Moreno, in Los
Angeles. He was ninety-three years of age. His friend,
Henry D. Barrows, left this lasting impression:

> All who came into social or business relations with the vener-
> able ex-Governor spontaneously bear witness to the kindness of
> his heart, to his uniform courtesy, and to his entire lack of malice
> or ill-will towards any human being.

Prior to his death, Pío Pico in 1877 preserved for
posterity the memory of his revolutionary years by dic-

tating two hundred pages of manuscript to Thomas
Savage. Savage at that time was collecting recollections
of *Californios* for the H. H. Bancroft collection. His-
torians since have made use of this "Narración His-
tórica" principally to satisfy references, but no attempt
was made for a complete translation and publication.
Had this been done in the 1920s when the significance
of Pico's life was becoming more and more apparent,
the colorful legends would not have succeeded. Lacking a foil, the pens of romance turned out stories that
in time became largely accepted as incidents of history.

Some years ago the Governor Pico Mansion Society
– an organization that concerns itself with the Pico
Mansion – felt a need to make Pico's autobiographical
narrative available to the public. Permission was received from the Bancroft Library to translate from
photocopies, and publish the account in English. The
late Arthur Botello, a long-time president of the Society, began the translating, a task that extended over a
period of several years of part-time devotion.

Art Botello, a descendant of a California first family,
had a deep, ingrained awareness of the culture and
mores of Pico's day, and consequently, the precious
flavor of the past was not lost in his translation. Because
Art was most meticulous, he was not satisfied with his
work until he had accomplished several drafts. Thus
time and effort brought about an outstanding literary
chronicle.

The reader will find the memoirs rambling and dis-
jointed, but be mindful that these are recollections of a
seventy-six-year-old man, well past the prime of life.
There are incidents set down not in chronological order,

so it must be presumed that, while reminiscing, he sometimes recalled an event that should have been mentioned previously. Savage made no attempt to rearrange the narrative, and thus we have it today, precisely as it was told by Pico. Headings have been editorially inserted in the text to aid in text divisions.

Regarding the annotations – Henry Welcome and myself did the toiling in the thorny vineyards of research, relying mainly on Bancroft's *History of California,* yet often cross-checking with the California histories of Eldredge and Hittell and others, and making use too of more recent publications such as Cowan's *Ranchos of California.*

Leola Butler also toiled in a supporting role as secretary of the Governor Pico Mansion Society, as did my wife, Ruth, as treasurer. They worked untiringly with the late Arthur Botello, and with Henry Welcome, our vice-president, and myself to accomplish a goal which the membership decided upon ages (it seems) ago.

Regarding the American period of Pico's life, may I refer the interested reader to my own publication, *Pío Pico Mansion: Fact, Fiction and Supposition.* Unfortunately this slim booklet is out of print, but copies are to be found in many libraries, and the material may also be found in the July 1963 issue of *Journal of the West.*

MARTIN COLE
President, Governor Pico
Mansion Society
formerly Curator, Pío Pico
State Historical Monument

Whittier, California, 1973

Historical Narrative
dictated to Thomas Savage
Los Angeles, October 24, 1877

THE EARLY YEARS

I was born on the 5th of May 1801, at the San Gabriel Mission where my father, José María Pico, company corporal of the San Diego garrison, commanded the cavalry. My father was a native of Fuerte,[1] at that time in the province of Sinaloa. My mother's name was María Eustaquia Gutiérrez, a native of San Miguel de Horcasitas[2] in Sonora.

My father had four brothers in California, namely: José Dolores,[3] who was a sergeant of the Monterey

---

[1] Fuerte, Mexico, in north central Sinaloa, close to the Sonora border.

[2] Horcasitas, Sonora, is the settlement from which Juan de Anza's colonizing expedition departed on September 29, 1775. At that time San Miguel de Horcasitas was the resident town of the governor of Sonora.

[3] José Dolores Pico was a Mexican soldier, who came to California about 1790; he married Gertrudis Amezquita in 1791, and served in the Santa Barbara Company to 1795, or later. Before 1804 he was transferred to the Monterey Company, here he married for the second time, the new bride being Isabel Cota. From 1811 he was sergeant of the company, being dangerously wounded in 1815. In 1819, he obtained a grant of the Bolsa de San Cayetano Rancho (Monterey County) and was in charge of the Rancho Nacional, Salinas, from 1821. He died in 1827, leaving a good record as a soldier and Indian fighter, though he lacked the education or birth which might have given him promotion. He was the founder of the northern branch of the Pico family. Antonio María and José de Jesus were the most prominent of his sons. There were thirteen children.

Company; Patricio, whom I knew as a rancher at the Simí ranch; Javier and Miguel,[4] soldiers at Santa Barbara.

My mother had here two half-brothers and four half-sisters, all born from the second marriage of my grandmother and bearing the surname López, namely: Ignacio and José who were soldiers of the San Diego Company; Josefa, married to a Mexican named Véjar, a carpenter in San Diego; Juliana, married to Juan Osuna, a corporal of the San Diego Company – Osuna later on was majordomo of the San Diego Mission much before the secularization; María Antonia, married to a soldier from San Diego named Jóse María Aguilar, mason by trade and, after being licensed, practicing this at the missions of San Luis Rey and San Juan Capistrano; María Ignacia, married to Joaquín Carrillo, also a soldier of the San Diego Company. A daughter of this half-aunt of mine married Don Mariano Guadalupe Vallejo. Another daughter married his brother, Don Salvador, and still another married Capt. Romualdo Pacheco and were the parents of our ex-governor Pacheco.

I had two brothers, José Antonio[5] and Andrés;[6] seven

4 The three Pico brothers, Francisco Javier, Miguel and Patricio were granted Rancho San José de García de Simí in years 1795 and 1821. These fourteen leagues of land lie in present day Ventura and Los Angeles counties.

5 José Antonio Pico, son of José María, was born at San Diego in 1794. About 1815 he enlisted in the San Diego Company; he is mentioned as a clerk in 1817, and in 1828, the sergeant of the company. He was charged with conspiracy in 1834, was promoted to alférez in 1834, and agent to secularize San Juan Capistrano. In 1836-38 Pico was transferred to the Monterey Company; promoted to lieutenant in 1838, then transferred to the Monterey Company at Sonoma. He left the military service in 1843, becoming grantee of Agua Caliente, San Diego County, in 1840, also of Rancho San Luis Rey in 1846. Nothing is heard of him in the troubles of 1845-48, but he continued to live in the south, dying at San Diego in 1871.

sisters:[7] Concepción, Tomasa, María, Isidora, Estéfana, Jacinta, and Feliciana, all of them married.

[6] Andrés Pico, son of José María, was born at San Diego in 1810. His first appearance in the public records is in 1836-38, when he was in charge of Jamul Rancho (San Diego County), also an elector and receptor of customs at San Diego. During the same period he took an active part on behalf of the south in the sectional political strife against the Monterey government, being half a dozen times a prisoner in that play of warfare and diplomacy. In 1839-42, his rank was alférez of the San Diego Company. For a time he was in charge of Mission San Luis Rey. He obtained lands at Santa Margarita, San Juan Capistrano (San Diego County) and Temecula. Pico was sent to Mexico in 1844 by Governor Micheltorena to obtain funds, and after his return devoted himself to military duties, as first lieutenant, then captain. He organized the militia at Los Angeles. In 1845 he was obliged to join the revolutionists and was in military command for a time at Monterey and also at Los Angeles. Aside from military duties, he was commissioned to take inventories of mission properties, and his land holdings included lessee of San Fernando and purchaser of Mission San Jose. In 1846, during the Mexican War, Pico ranked captain of the regular company, then became chief command on the flight of Castro; at one stage of the war he surrendered to the Americans, and was paroled, but broke his parole to serve with Flores. He was in command of the *Californios* at the Battle of San Pascual – this was the most notable achievement of his life. Following the Battle of San Gabriel at war's end, where he commanded the cavalry, he signed the Treaty of Cahuenga with Fremont, thus closing the war in California. In 1848-49, Pico had a company of miners at work on the Mokelumne. He was elected to the California assembly in 1851, and state senator in 1860-61. Much of his time in later years was devoted to land litigation, especially in connection with his San Fernando estate. He died in 1876. Bancroft states: "Andrés Pico was a brave, reckless, coarse grained, jovial, kind-hearted, popular man; abler in several respects than his brother Don Pío, but not over burdened with principle. He never married."

[7] José María Pico, brother of José Dolores, son of Santiago Pico of Fuerte, Sinaloa, was the founder of the Pico family in Southern California. He was a soldier of the San Diego Company from 1782, corporal of the guard at San Luis Rey from 1798, and sergeant 1805-18, being retired with perhaps a brevet rank of alférez. He died in 1819 at San Gabriel, where he had long been in command of the guard. His marriage in 1789 was to María Eustaquia López. (Pío Pico stated María Eustaquia Gutiérrez was his mother's maiden name. His maternal grandmother bore the name of López only after a subsequent marriage.) The three sons of José, namely, José Antonio, Andrés and Pío appear in the Bancroft *Pioneer Register,* together with seven daughters. They married: Concepción to Domingo Carrillo, Estéfana to José Antonio Carrillo, and following Estéfana's death, Jacinta married José Antonio Carrillo, Tomasa to Francisco Alvarado, and Feliciana to José Ramón Argüello.

I was raised in San Diego. An old lady named Ma-
tilde Carrillo, wife of Joaquín Arce,[8] sergeant of San
Diego, taught me to read, and when I was about twelve
years old, more or less, Don José Antonio Carrillo, who
was my brother-in-law, having been the husband of two
of my sisters, taught me to write.

Señor Carrillo had me draw lines on paper and then
he would write from one margin to the other "Señor
Don Félix María Callejas" so I could copy it. He never
gave me other words and I do not know how many
reams of paper I filled with those same words.

Señor Carrillo at that time had a kind of school at
the presidio of San Diego attended by daughters of
some friends and also some soldiers who had been
named corporals. I knew three or four others who went
there to learn to write.

I continued at my mother's side without leaving her
except to attend to business.

The year 1812, the church of San Juan Capistrano
fell down as the consequence of some strong earth-
quakes.[9]

The year 1811, a conspiracy among the troops in San
Diego was discovered.[10] My father was a sergeant of

---

[8] Sergeant Arce was one of the leading characters in the comic-opera naval
"Battle of San Diego." In March of 1803 the American brig "Lelia Byrd"
sailed into San Diego Bay to attempt illegal smuggling and trading of furs.
The Mexican authorities placed Arce with five men aboard a two-master to
prevent lawbreaking.

[9] On December 8, 1812, a great earthquake at San Juan Capistrano undid
the construction work of years, and killed forty neophytes. The collapsed
church was never rebuilt.

[10] In 1811 some sixty men and officers plotted to seize the post. Before reaching a point of action, the conspiritors, including Sergeant José Pico, were
arrested. Henry D. Barrows in an 1881 interview with Pío Pico was told,
"I remember that in 1810, my father was put in prison on account of the talk,
in the company of which he was sergeant, of Mexican independence, a ques-

the company and was accused of being involved in the movement. He was confined to quarters. Also taken prisoners and put in chains were four [sic] soldiers of the company of leatherjackets: Ramón Rubio, José María López, García, Canedo, and an artilleryman named Ignacio Zúñiga. Three of the soldiers died chained in the same quarters – of course, they had been imprisoned many years. Artilleryman Zúñiga was in chains until independence was achieved. The soldier García was set at liberty at the conclusion of the affair.

In the year 1813, there was an Indian insurrection at the San Gabriel Mission.[11] The garrison companies were moved, part of the four companies going to San Gabriel. If my memory is correct, the troops from the north arrived commanded by Ensign Gabriel Moraga.[12] Those from San Diego came commanded by my father who placed himself under the orders of officer Moraga. The rebellious Indians took part of a herd of sheep and

---

tion which was, even then, much agitated throughout Mexico. He was released, after a few days, through the influence of the missionary fathers, but the soldiers, Ramón Rubio, José M. López, and one, Canedo, and an artilleryman, Ygnacio Zúñiga, were kept in confinement, each with two pairs of irons (grillos), the two first-named dying in prison and Zúñiga remaining there in irons until Mexican independence was established in 1821."

[11] The Indian raiding parties of the Mohave Desert and beyond, filtered into Southern California by way of the Cajon Pass. The raids increased during the mission period as the establishments of the padres provided more useful products to steal. The cattle and horses were especially vulnerable. Converts (neophytes) were not above assisting their wild cousins. In time the raiding parties grew larger and more cunning. Once the San Gabriel Mission reported eight hundred Yumas headed over the pass, their intent this time, was to destroy both San Gabriel and San Fernando missions. Fortunately, military reinforcements prevented the attack.

[12] Gabriel Moraga, in 1776, was a boy when he arrived with his parents. He enlisted in 1784 and progressed through the ranks – soldier, corporal, sergeant, alférez and finally lieutenant of the San Francisco, Monterey, and Santa Barbara companies until his death in 1823. (According to Bancroft, the rank "alférez" is interchangable with "ensign.")

other things to the mountains. They were pursued by the troops and quite a few of the things were recovered. Some of the Indians were brought back to the mission. Of these, some were taken to San Diego. Nearly all of the prisoners were whipped and those that lived remained in prison at San Diego until their deaths.

We were told by our father that at the battle in the mountains a handsome Indian (one of those taken to San Diego) fought heroically, wounding two of the soldiers. He was finally taken with great difficulty because he barricaded himself behind dead bodies. Four of his bows had been broken by shots but he continued the struggle. My father instructed the troops that he not be killed if he could be taken alive. And so it was done, but afterwards he was known as Bonaparte.

In 1815, my father came with the commandant's permission to await his retirement [papers] at San Gabriel.

The year 1818, when Bouchard's [13] insurgent expedition came, the commandant called him to San Diego,

13 Hippolyte de Bouchard, a Frenchman by birth, commanded two Argentine war ships serving in Mexico's War of Independence with Spain. California regarded as favoring Spain was thus the object of a hit-and-run commando raid. After outfitting his ships in Hawaii, Bouchard reached Monterey on November 20, 1818. With a large landing party he managed to take the town on the 22nd. The local people followed by the defending soldiers had fled inland to distant Mission Soledad for refuge. By the 27th the insurgents had repaired damage that the *Californio* artillery, before retreating, inflicted on their smaller ship. After setting fire to the fort and presidio, Bouchard sailed southward and made a brief landing on December 2nd at Refugio, some twenty miles west of Santa Barbara. Finding the ranch house deserted the party plundered and burned the building, however, a force of *Californios* managed to capture three of the invaders. Bouchard next anchored off Santa Barbara to negotiate for these men, and succeeded in making a trade. He again sailed southward, and on December 14th, anchored off San Juan Capistrano. Reinforcements under Alférez Santiago Argüello arrived from San Diego, while a party was ashore for supplies. Argüello's show of strength prompted a return to their ship. Four deserters were found after the ships sailed.

placing in his [my father's] charge the force located on
the esplanade of the fortification to defend it in case
the enemy came to invade. He remained there until the
insurgents left and there was no more danger.

Bouchard's insurgents disembarked first at Monterey,
burning the presidio and plundering everything of
value. They then disembarked in Refugio, plundering
it. Then they were in Santa Barbara but did no harm
there. From there they went to San Juan Capistrano
and took everything they found in storage, including
the church's silver ornaments. They then continued
their voyage, passing San Diego without stopping at the
port, and nothing more was heard of them.

During my father's absence in San Diego, I was left
in charge of the guard at San Gabriel which was com-
prised of residents of Los Angeles.

The campaign having ended, my father again returned to San Gabriel commanding the guard com-
prised of fifteen soldiers. This was not customary as the
missions' guards were usually made up of four soldiers
and a corporal.

My father did not succeed in being retired as a
veteran. He continued in active service until his death,
which was in September of 1819.

After the death of my father all the family moved to
San Diego. Nothing was left us – not even an inch of
ground. My older brother, José Antonio, was already in
service but the rest of my family, except for two sisters
already married, stayed at my mother's side and I had
to solicit help for her. My sisters and my mother
worked at fine needlework. My sister, Tomasa, always
finished before the rest because of her expertness.

I put up a small store where I sold liquors, provisions, chairs, and shoes. I always had a clerk in the store because I frequently went to Los Angeles and the missions and as far as the border of Baja California to sell goods and to bring back cattle and other goods in exchange.

One time I left San Diego with a load of sugar for the border of Baja California. Arriving at San Vicente,[14] I lodged in the house of Lieutenant Commander Don Manuel Ruiz, brother of Francisco María.[15] While there, I visited the *Padre Ministre* [Father Minister] of the San Vicente Mission, Fr. Antonio Menendez,[16] and the padre invited me to play a game of cards. I accepted. We played and he won all the sugar. I did not know the game and I had no idea that the priest would win, but he did and I returned to my home with nothing. When I turned over the sugar to him, Father Menendez said to me: "See here, Pico, it has happened to you as it did to Christ when he came into the world." I asked, "What happened to Christ?" and he responded: "Christ came into the world to redeem

---

14 Historian Henry Welcome believes Pío Pico was referring to the old Spanish and Mexican boundary between the two Californias, located some thirty miles south of the present international line. San Vicente, Baja California, is a good 130 miles south of San Diego by the present highway. Pío Pico, no doubt, traveled farther by trail.

15 Francisco María Ruiz, a native of Baja California, was in turn sergeant of the Santa Barbara Company from 1795, alférez 1801, lieutenant 1805 and from 1806 comandant at San Diego, being promoted to captain in 1820 and retired from active service in 1827. He received a grant of the Peñasquitos Rancho (Santa María de Peñasquitos, San Diego County, northeast of La Jolla. Ruiz was claimant for 8,486 acres, granted in 1824 and 1834). He died in 1839 at the age of eighty-five. He never married.

16 Father Antonio Menendez came to California in 1825. He had been a Spanish Dominican friar on the Lower California frontier, was relieved from missionary work for irregular conduct (gambling perhaps?), and became employed as chaplain of the troops at San Diego in 1825.

sinners. He came for wool and left shorn. You came to sell your sugar and now leave penniless."

This same Father Menendez some years later was chaplain of the San Diego Company and parson of the town. Still later he was transferred to Los Angeles and thence to Monterey.

During the stay of the padre in San Diego, we again played and I won from him twelve mules which he had brought from Baja California. I then told him: "Father, I do not want to behave like a tyrant. I will return your saddled black mule" and that is what I did.

My mother never knew of my adventure in San Vicente with Father Menendez but my sister Tomasa did. She was my confidante and took care of my money.

Tomasa once loaned $30.00 to a soldier from Baja California. I came home and my sister asked me if I had seen the soldier. I answered that I knew the soldier had left for Baja. She told me that the soldier owed her $30.00 and I offered to go and catch up with him. I went immediately. I caught up with him at Rancho de la Nación,[17] about eight leagues [18] from San Diego, and he paid me the $30.00. After paying me he invited me to play. On the ranch was a corporal and four soldiers whose duty it was to watch after the interest of La Nación. The corporal liked me very much and urged me to play with the soldier. He carried quite a bit of money * from Monterey and Los Angeles. I won all

[17] Rancho de la Nación, San Diego County, at National City and Chula Vista. Six leagues were granted in 1845 to John Forster, who was claimant for 26,632 acres, patented February 27, 1866. This area was originally grazing lands owned by the San Diego Mission; in 1795-1845 it was used by the military of the San Diego presidio.

[18] A Spanish league is about 2.6 miles. An English league is three miles.

* The word used is *intereses,* literally: interest – money paid for the use of money.

that he carried. The soldier had on a pair of corduroy pants trimmed with gold thread. I asked him if he had anything more with which to play and he answered that he had only his pants and, if I wished, he would wager them. I did not want to play for his pants but my friend, the corporal, pursuaded me to do so. With the pants, he not only won back all my money but my sister's $30.00.

Afterwards, he continued playing with the corporal and the four soldiers and left them all bare. He did not even leave them the buttons on their uniforms. He won even their leather pants.

At that time I was about twenty-three years old and I had never been interested in things political. My mother was very strict with me and never allowed me to be away from home after 8 o'clock at night, and until I was twenty-five I observed this rule.

As a young child I was quite advanced in praying. I knew all Ripalda's catechism from beginning to end and when new people would arrive from Mexico, Don José Antonio Carrillo's mother [19] would call me and I would recite all the catechism with my arms crossed. This brought me much praise. Also, at the San Diego Mission, Father Fernando Martínez – a man of little culture – had me assist at mass in Latin without me understanding one word of what he was saying.

Turning back to the year 1798, my father came as a corporal when San Luis Rey was founded, and there my sister, Tomasa, was born while the mission was being built in 1799. The year 1801, as I said before, he moved to San Gabriel where I was born in a shack made of

---

[19] Tomasa Ignacia Carrillo (nee Lugo) was the wife of José Raimundo Carrillo, and mother of Don José Antonio Carrillo. Tomasa and her husband are regarded as the founders of the Carrillo family in California.

branches, there being no houses. At the time, there lived in San Gabriel a Señora Eulalia Pérez,[20] who is now about 125 years old and who had come in her youth from Sonora with her husband, the soldier Guillén, of the San Diego Company. This lady acted as midwife at my mother's childbirth.

The year 1821, I left here for the town of San José Guadalupe[21] in charge of a shipment of barrels of wine and *aguardiente*[22] that Don José Antonio Carrillo was sending from Los Angeles as a gift to fathers Luis Martínez[23] of San Luis Obispo, and Juan Cabot[24] of San Miguel. After delivering the goods in San Miguel, I went on to Monterey with five barrels of aguardiente that I had of my own. I arrived at the Rancho Nacional[25] and met my uncle, José Dolores Pico, who had it in his care. From the ranch I went to San José with my barrels. There I stayed in the company of Señor Ignacio Vallejo,[26] brother of the general, arrang-

---

[20] Eulalia Pérez de Guillén is often referred to as living to be 140 years of age. For example, the January 1929 issue of *Touring Topics* (now *Westways*) attempts to offer proof. Despite such publicity there is good evidence she nevei reached the century mark. She died at San Gabriel on February 8th, 1878. Bancroft allows her a possible 104 years at time of her death.

[21] San José Guadalupe was the first Spanish pueblo in Alta California. In time the name was shortened to San José.

[22] Aguardiente, at that time, a poorly distilled brandy, usually made from grapes.

[23] Father Luis Antonio Martínez of San Luis Obispo Mission. He came as a Spanish friar to California in 1798 and served at San Luis Obispo Mission for thirty-two years. He was banished in 1830 for alleged complicity in the Solis revolt.

[24] Juan Cabot was a Spanish priest who came to California in 1805 and served for thirty years, mostly at San Miguel Mission. He retired to his college in 1835.

[25] Rancho Nacional, of two leagues, is located in Monterey County at the north edge of Salinas on the river of same name. It was granted in 1839 to Vicente Cantua, who was claimant for 6,633 acres. Pío Pico's uncle became caretaker of the rancho that year.

ing the sale of the aguardiente. He was about eighteen years old, more or less. I stayed in San José three or four months and, when my aguardiente was sold, I returned to San Diego.

The year 1826, if I remember right, I was a voting member of the Deputation [vocal de la Diputación] but it was not in session and the members [vocales] did not have a single privilege unless the chamber [la cámara] was in session.

In 1827 or 1828, I was named scribe or secretary to

---

26 Young Ignacio Vallejo is not included in the *Pioneer Register*. Bancroft only mentions the four of the elder Ignacio's five sons. These four survived the father who died in 1831. The younger Ignacio may have died before his father. Zoeth S. Eldredge in his *Beginnings of San Francisco* indicates the younger Ignacio was born in 1795, this would make him about twenty-six when Pico visited.

The following is quoted from Henry T. Barrows', "Pío Pico," in the *Annual Publication of the Historical Society of Southern California for 1894*. For Barrows information, Pico recalled: "In 1821 I was employed by my brother-in-law, José Antonio Carrillo, to take twenty-five barrels of liquor to the northern part of the Territory to distribute to the fathers at the missions, as a particular present to them from him, the same being, at that time, liquor of the first quality. Señor Carrillo was then one of the most influential and capable men in California. . .

"Being, as I said, charged to take the liquor up the country, I contracted with an old man (un anciano) named Encarnación Urquidez, grandfather of Mrs. Governor Downey, for twenty-five mules, and engaged three men, citizens of the Pueblo. . . On my way northward I made a short visit to the Presidio of Monterey, accompanied by a cousin, Jesús Pico. The first house I visited was that of Don Ygnacio Vallejo, father of the Vallejo of the North. I then paid my respects to Governor Vicente Sola, who received me with much courtesy and kindness (amabilidad) ; only he was surprised to see me wearing a military uniform. I explained to him that my father had died whilst in the military service, leaving his uniform to me, and that therefore I was by right entitled to use it in the form he left it. I remember that on my reply he drew near me, and, placing his hand on my shoulder, he said to me that I could enjoy my military privileges (fuero militar), and he gave me a recommendatory letter to the Comandante at San Diego, who reported in my favor, and I was afterwards appointed Lieutenant of the militia." Pío Pico was twenty at the time.

Captain Don Pablo de la Portilla,[27] who was named attorney-general, to take down declarations from one Señor Bringas,[28] a Mexican.

[27] Captain Pablo Portilla, at the time Pico assisted him, was stationed in San Diego and in charge of military trials.

[28] In connection with Herrera's trial in 1827, Bancroft states: "In April 1827 (Governor) Echeandía ordered a secret investigation on Herrera's administration, to be conducted by Zamorano. The proceedings were begun at San Diego on the 30th of April, and afterwards continued at Monterey and Los Angeles in May and June. The main charge was that the comisario had, on his way to California, invested a portion of the $22,000 of territorial funds entrusted to his care in effects to be sold for his own account and profit, though it was not claimed apparently that there was any deficit in his accounts, or that money thus improperly used had not been refunded. Zamorano as fiscal reported the charge well founded. . . We consider that these proceedings were conducted in secret, mainly by Herrera's enemies, that they were never carried further in public, that Herrera was never called upon for a defense upon any criminal charge . . . it would seem wisest at the least to attach little importance to the accusations."

Henry T. Barrows "Pío Pico" article *(loc. cit.)* offers further information: "In the year 1828 I was appointed Secretary in a suit which Captain Pablo de la Portilla came (from San Diego to Los Angeles), on order of General José M. Estudillo, to try, against a Mexican citizen named Luis Bringas. We arrived at the Pueblo, and the Captain established his office in a building on the site of the present jail (now the Phillips Block on North Spring Street), owned by Antonio Rocha, a Portuguese. The next day Bringas was cited and appeared before Captain de la Portilla. Being asked what he had to say to the charges brought by the Captain, he refused to answer or plead, saying that no Mexican citizen ought to answer before any military authority (y que como militar, le componia tanto como si fuera la suela de su zapata), and that it would be a very great outrage for a civilian to be tried by a military tribunal; that Mexican citizens constituted the sacred base (base sagrada) of the nation; that it was they who formed the nation, and not the military; and that for these reasons he refused to answer (declarar). Seeing that he was resolute, Captain de la Portilla determined to place the refusal of Bringas before the General Comandante at San Diego. His communication to this effect having been prepared, I offered to carry the documents, and I left immediately for San Diego, where I placed the same in the hands of the Comandante, Don José M. Estudillo; he received and hurriedly examined them, when he ordered me to retire to my residence, and to return the next day at 10 a.m., to take back his answer.

"Having myself learned, meanwhile, the purport of the allegations of Señor Bringas, and understanding the rights which he showed that Mexican citizens

Señor Bringas was a merchant established in Los
Angeles and it was said that the merchandise he sold
belonged to Don José María Herrera, principal sub-
commissioner residing in Monterey, who was accused
of misappropriation of public funds and of having purchased this merchandise with government money which
had been given him in Mexico to pay the troops in
California.

Captain Portilla and I arrived at Los Angeles and
arranged a meeting with Señor Bringas at an office that
had been established by the captain in the home of Don
Antonio Rocha, situated where the city jail [29] is now.
Señor Bringas presented himself. The captain informed
him of the object of his commission, at which Bringas
answered that he respected and esteemed him very much
as a private individual and as a friend, but as a captain
of the Mexican Army he was nothing more to him than
the sole of his shoe. This reply impressed me pro-
foundly because we considered a captain a personage of
high rank and distinction. Not only captains, but all

possessed, I was so impressed thereby that on the next day, when I presented
myself before the Comandante, Estudillo, I was resolved to make known my
rights as a citizen, which in effect, I did.

"On appearing before the Comandante, he delivered to me the documents,
with the order for me to take them back to Los Angeles to Captain de la
Portilla. I refused to obey the order, alleging that I was a citizen, and that
therefore, the military authorities had no jurisdiction over me. Whereupon I
was thrown into prison, where I remained one day and one night.

"The next day the Comandante called me before him, and I had the satisfaction of being publicly set at liberty. From that date I began to know the
sacred rights of a citizen."

29 The city jail was on the west side of Spring Street almost directly across
from the main entrance to the present Los Angeles City Hall. Harris Newmark in his *Sixty Years in Southern California* says on page 530, "Again
obliged to seek more room, the Phillips Block, at the corner of Spring and
Franklin streets, was built for their use on the site of the old City and County
Building and the Jail." Franklin ran from Spring Street to Broadway.

officials and even sergeants and corporals and even the lowest of soldiers were treated with consideration.

I was even more surprised when I heard Bringas tell Portilla that the civilians [paisanos] were the sacred core of the nation, and that the military were nothing more than servants of the nation, which was constituted of the people and not of the military. Bringas declared he would not give his statement except in front of a person in civil authority, even though he were an Indian *alcalde* from the mission. But not before a military man, whatever his rank. Convinced, Señor Portilla decided to send a message to the commandant general and another to the commandant of San Diego Captain José María Estudillo,[30] laying before them Bringas' reluctance.

I offered to take the communication to the commandant of San Diego and my offer was accepted. I arrived at San Diego and delivered the document and was told by Señor Estudillo that I should go to my home to rest until the next day, and that I should return to take the reply back to Los Angeles. By then I was beginning to feel the effects of Señor Bringas' words.

My mother and my family were all in need of my services in San Diego and made it plain to me that for this reason, they were opposed to my return to Los Angeles. I wanted to please my mother and at the same time show my sense of independence. I now considered myself a "sacred vessel" – words which sounded very good to my ears. I presented myself to Estudillo. He

[30] Captain José María Estudillo was a Spanish lieutenant of the Monterey Company who came to California in 1806 and served at Monterey until 1827 when he became captain of the San Diego Company. He died in 1830, having founded the Estudillo family of California. (Note: Barrows' footnote 28 is in error, listing Estudillo as a general.)

had the official letter ready in his hand and he asked
me if I was prepared to depart as he handed me the
letter. I told him that I was not able to return to Los
Angeles as I was needed at home. Then Señor Estudillo
issued orders to the sergeant that I should be taken to
the jail. They imprisoned me in a cell with other prisoners though I had the luck not to be placed in irons.
I was there all that day and that night and the next
morning Estudillo ordered my release, and that I
should be taken to the commandant's office. I went there
and he asked me to excuse the manner in which I had
been treated – that it had been a hot-headed action and
that I should go and look after my mother. I retired to
my home and stayed at my mother's side, but always it
appeared to me, deep in my soul, that the citizens were
the nation and that no military was superior to us.

ECHEANDIA'S ADMINISTRATION

About that time, Commandant General Echeandía[31]
was in Monterey, returning to San Diego shortly thereafter. This was probably in June or July 1828. The territorial Chamber of Deputies, of which I was a member, was brought together. When the chamber convened, I proposed that we dispose of the matter discussed at a previous session: that of establishing Los
Angeles as capital of the territory. The chamber was so
disposed, as Los Angeles was the older and more pop-
ulous town, while Monterey and the other presidios
were nothing more than military posts.

The meeting of the chamber had a quorum. Present

---

31 José María Echeandía came to California in 1825 with appointment of
Governor and Commanding General of the Californias; he made San Diego
his headquarters and the capital. His governorship was from November 1825
to the end of January 1831, when he was replaced by Manuel Victoria.

were four *vocales* and the *Jefe Político*.[32] (The *jefe político* had a voice in the discussions and two votes in the decision.) I insisted that if the chamber did not move to Los Angeles to have its sessions, I would return to my home. As this was not done, I returned home and the chamber was left without a quorum, and so was dissolved by the *jefe político*.

At that time, the question was raised whether it was necessary for the *jefe político* to be present, presiding over the chamber. I maintained it was not needed because if he wasn't present, the eldest *vocal* could preside over the session.

The following procedure was observed in the election of deputies: The voters were the neighboring townspeople who chose the electors. These elected the deputies, each of whom had, and were required to have, $4,000.00 worth of property. Of the prior chamber, there always remained two for the following. The electors established the post of each deputy, designating if the elected was first, second, third, etc., but always keeping in mind that the ones remaining from the previous chamber should be the senior members. That is, if there should remain from the previous chamber numbers six and seven, these were advanced immediately to numbers one and two.

I was of the opinion that if the military matters of the *jefe político* required it, he should remain in San Diego; that the Territorial *Diputación* had nothing to

---

[32] In this case jefe político means governor. Zoeth S. Eldredge in his *Beginnings of San Francisco* says of Pío Pico, "He headed a revolt against Governor Victoria in 1831 and on the overthrow of that official was named by the diputación, "jefe político" (governor) ad interim, January 11, 1832." Pico felt the territorial Chamber of Deputies could meet and function without the jefe político as long as it had a quorum.

do with military affairs. But I could accomplish nothing. The chamber was dissolved and the *jefe político* arranged that the deputation be established in Monterey and not at Los Angeles. He sent out circulars to the proprietary deputies and alternates. Because of that, I set out for Monterey where the alternates met. No proprietary deputies were present other than Don José Tiburcio Castro[33] and I. I was in Monterey three or four days and then decided to send a communication to the alternate deputies so that we might constitute the chamber. We reconvened and I presided over the chamber as the senior *vocal*. This was in 1828 and I was about twenty-eight years old.

The alternate members that took office were Don Carlos Castro, Don Joaquín and Don Antonio Buelna.[34] The chamber lacked a quorum since it was not patent whether there was a legitimate reason for the non-attendance of the proprietary members. I brought this to the notice of those attending and then we dissolved. I departed for San Diego and gave the *jefe político* my account.

In the year 1829, as a consequence of a revolt of the troops headed by Joaquín Solís,[35] the general left San

[33] Castro was a representative from San José. He was also the father of the José Castro (see note 84).

[34] Carlos Castro was no relation of José Tiburcio Castro, but must have filled in for the absent José Tiburcio. José Joaquín Estudillo was a son of José María Estudillo. Antonio Buelna was from Monterey.

[35] Joaquín Solís was a Mexican convict who was exiled to California in 1825. Due to lack of pay and poor rations, the soldiers at the Monterey Presidio revolted on the night of November 12th, 1829. Seeking a leader, they chose Solís who was ranching near the town. He in turn supposedly petitioned Governor Echeandía to correct existing evils, but he plead his cause through José Herrera, the governor's old enemy. Three nights later a plan was read to a group of local foreigners, who were mainly Americans. Herrera's guiding hand was in this declaration of revolution and some of his personal grievances

Diego for Santa Barbara, notifying the proprietary deputies that they should convene at Santa Barbara. There, the chamber was installed, presided over by *Jefe Político* Echeandía who issued a statement that in view of the critical circumstances existing in the country, they had called us there to help pacify the country. We all cooperated with great pleasure.

Upon arriving in the vicinity of Cieneguita,[36] the revolutionaries with Solís disbanded and returned in disorder to Monterey. Solís and his companions found as they neared Monterey that the garrison they had left there had turned in favor of the government.

After this episode was concluded, the chamber dissolved and the deputies returned to their homes. That happened in the beginning of 1830.

When we received notice that the new *jefe político* and commandant-general, Lieutenant Colonel Don Manuel Victoria,[37] was expected, I went out to meet him about eight leagues from San Diego. There he gave me a letter of recommendation that had been given to him for me by my merchant friend, Don Enrique Virmond.[38]

---

were included. Echeandía was accused by the group as responsible for all local problems.

[36] Cieneguita, should be Cieneguitas. An area full of springs and swampland a few miles west of Santa Barbara. The grant of Suerte en las Cieneguitas also known as Paraje de las Cieneguitas was made to Anastasio Carrillo in 1845.

[37] Manuel Victoria was appointed in Mexico City to replace Echeandía. The lieutenant-colonel arrived in California late in 1830, taking over the governorship at the end of January 1831. Within the year he too was disposed by a revolutionary movement led by Pío Pico and Echeandía. Victoria left California on January 17, 1832, embarking from San Diego on the American ship "Pocahontas," sailing for San Blas.

[38] Henry Virmond visited California during the years 1828-1830. He was a German merchant with offices in Acapulco and Mexico City, and much of his trade was in California. His name was well known to nearly everyone before

Don José María de Echeandía was a man of about
forty-eight years, tall, slender, fair, black hair, small
beard and of pleasant manner. He was not haughty, but
he was very apathetic and, as a result, crimes became
common. He was the one that initiated the secularization of the missions.

During the administration of Echeandía, there occurred the curious incident of the marriage of the American, Captain Henry D. Fitch[39] and my first cousin,
Josefa Carrillo.

Fitch, with the intention of marrying Josefa[40] after
getting the consent of her parents, was baptized and
joined the Catholic Church. All preparations had been
made and present to witness the marriage rites were
Father Antonio Menendez, the bride and groom, the
sponsors who were Don Domingo Carrillo[41] and the
narrator, and my sister Isidora. The day before, Señor
Echeandía had issued an order to the priest that they
could not be married because Fitch was a foreigner and
not a naturalized Mexican. The following day, Captain Fitch went out to sea in his boat, hanging around

his first arrival, partly because he was the tallest man seen in California until
Dr. Semple arrived in 1845. Some comparison may be made in knowing that
Semple was about six feet, eight inches.

[39] Captain Henry Delano Fitch was born at New Bedford, Mass., in 1799.
He came to California as the master of Virmond's brig, "María Ester." In
1827 he announced his intention of becoming a Mexican citizen and in 1829
was baptized at San Diego as Enrique Domingo Fitch.

[40] Doña Josefa was born at San Diego in 1810, and baptized María Antonia
Natalia Elijia Carrillo. Her father, a native of Baja California, was Joaquín
Carrillo, her mother, María Ignacia López. She was called Josefa later, when
her godmother forgot the names and thought one was Josefa! Pío's mother
had four half-sisters in California with the maiden name of López. Josefa was
Pío's half-cousin.

[41] Domingo Carrillo was the brother-in-law of Pío Pico, and husband of his
sister Concepción.

the port all day until at vespers that evening, my cousin, Josefa, arrived at my house and told me that she had agreed with Captain Fitch to go and get married in Valparaíso, and that she considered herself very unfortunate in not finding a person she could trust to take her to the appointed place to meet Fitch. Seeing her in such a plight, I offered to take her. Fortunately, it was a Friday in Lent and her mother had gone to church. I asked her if she was ready to depart. She replied affirmatively. I told her to go in back of her parents' house and I would come for her on horseback to take her to the pier. That was carried out without mishap. Just as we arrived at the pier, Fitch arrived in his boat. Josefa boarded the boat and I left. A few moments after I arrived home Josefa's parents became alarmed and began to look for her. Her father went to Echeandía to tell him that his daughter had left home and he did not know where she had gone. Echeandía suspected that Josefa and Fitch had gone away together. He sent a corporal and five soldiers at once to see if they could be found, but it was all in vain. The birds had flown.

Josefa Carrillo was a very beautiful young woman who danced very well. Echeandía always favored her at the dances.

Upon returning from their journey already married, they were forced to separate and to suffer other unpleasantness until the matter was brought before the ecclesiastical court which held the marriage valid.

GOVERNOR VICTORIA

Don Manuel Victoria was a tall man, somewhat hunchbacked, very dark, thin, beardless – his manner very gruff and despotic. I had little to do with him but in that short time I was aware of what I said above. Shortly after his arrival, he took over political and military authority. He immediately took a liking towards the person of the first *alcalde* [42] of Los Angeles, Don Vicente Sánchez, [43] who was also a member of the territorial deputation.

During his administration it was the general opinion that Victoria was a despotic ruler who did not want to recognize the right of the deputies to perform their duties. Therefore I, as a deputy, came to Los Angeles to consult with Vicente Sánchez. We were in agreement and we issued a communication to Victoria asking him to call a meeting because we had important matters to discuss. I signed the communication and gave it to Señor Sánchez for his signature, but he did not sign it and he sent the document to Victoria. He answered asking him to pursuade me not to concern myself in such matters as demanding a meeting of the deputation; that it was entirely up to the head of government to convene or not, in accordance with the instructions he had from the supreme government.

As a result of this communication, Victoria made a public speech. After this, I decided to give a reply as a *vocal* of the territorial deputation, as in effect I did,

42 Alcalde: mayor or head of city or town council (ayuntamiento – see footnote 44).

43 Vicente Sánchez was mayor of Los Angeles in 1830 when Pico arrived to consult with him. Few characters in history equaled him. Bancroft says, "In 1829-32 he as diputado, alcalde, and citizen was involved in a complicated series of troubles, being deposed and imprisoned, and in turn imprisoning others. The details cannot be presented, even if anybody understood them. He was a vicious, gambling, quarrelsome fellow, though of some intelligence and wealth; and political quarrels between Echeandía and Victoria had something to do with his trouble." Sánchez was the original grantee of Rancho Ciénega o Paso de la Tijera. He died in 1846.

having it circulated among the *ayuntamientos* [44] so that these might give it the most publicity.

The ayuntamiento of Monterey displayed my answer in their court of justice where all the people could see it. When Victoria learned of it, he ordered the ayuntamiento to remove it. That body refused to do so and then Victoria ordered Ensign Rodrigo del Pliego [45] with twenty-five men to go and tear down the document from the door of the town hall.

Alcalde Vicente Sánchez did not make public my manifesto and as I desired it to be made public, I sent a copy of it to my brother, Andrés, who was in Los Angeles. He gave it to many people to read, until it came to the attention of the alcalde, who demanded the document from my brother. He refused and the alcalde ordered him sent to jail, putting him in irons.

At that time, a brother-in-law of mine by the name of Joaquín Ortega [46] was in Monterey. He promptly came to tell me that General Victoria was making preparations to come down with troops to hang me, along with Don Juan Bandini,[47] who was also a resident of San

[44] Ayuntamiento corresponds to an American town council. It was composed of one alcalde, two regidores (council men) and a síndico-procurador (city attorney). In the largest towns the number of alcaldes and regidores were increased.

[45] Rodrigo Pliego came to California in 1825. He served as ensign in the Monterey, Santa Barbara and San Diego companies until 1831; he left California in 1832 with Victoria. (Note: The rank of ensign may be also referred to as alférez.)

[46] Joaquín Ortega was married to Pío Pico's sister, María.

[47] Juan Bandini, son of José, born in Lima, Peru, 1800, came to California as a young man in the middle 1820s. All his life he was quite active politically, socially, and in business. Death took him at the age of fifty-nine in Los Angeles. He is frequently mentioned in all works of California history, for this period.

Diego and whom Victoria had removed from his employment as sub-commissary.

Because of Alcalde Vicente Sánchez's misrepresentations, my brother-in-law, Don José Antonio Carrillo,[48] had been banished by Victoria to the border of Baja California. I was living at my ranch at Jamul.[49] I wrote Carrillo asking him to come to my ranch because I had important business to discuss with him. Carrillo came to my ranch and after we had a conference, we went to San Diego. As Carrillo could not appear publicly, we entered the town at night and I arranged for lodgings. That same night I went to look for Bandini, who came with me to where Carrillo was. During that interview we discussed the best methods to combat Victoria's plans. We resolved to plan an uprising.

Don José Antonio Carrillo shut himself up for eight or ten days while the plans were being prepared. In the conferences we had it decided that I should come to Los Angeles and invite the most notable persons to support our plans. I arrived in Los Angeles and learned that Alcalde Sánchez had about seventy of the most outstanding men (among them the *Regidor* Francisco Sepúlveda, Don José María Avila, Demesio Domínguez, and my brother in irons, and Nezario and Pedro Domínguez) in the public jail.

---

48 José Antonio Carrillo's first wife was Estefana Pico, and the second was Jacinta Pico.

49 Jamul Rancho is twenty-five miles southeast of San Diego on state highway 94. It was granted originally to Pío Pico in 1829 by Governor Echeandía and confirmed in 1831. The area is still very much as it was over a century ago, with beef cattle grazing on chaparral-covered hills, and the flat, sloping valleys are cultivated for dry farming of hay and grain. According to author Cecil C. Moyer, Jamul is an Indian word meaning "Slimy water." Alfred Kroeber says the name is Diegueño and means foam or lather.

Having great confidence in José María Avila[50] for his determination and courage, I decided to talk to him and reveal the scheme we were planning. I got close to the door of the cell in which he was confined and with much caution, I made known to him our plans. He was of the opinion that the ones from here should not revolt until Victoria had passed through to San Diego because he and his fellow prisoners believed that Victoria, upon his arrival in Los Angeles, would disapprove of the alcalde's action and would order them liberated and when Victoria should set out for San Diego to pursue me and the others, they would then rebel and would attack him from the rear.

I returned to San Diego and informed Carrillo and Bandini of it but we held to the idea of carrying out our plan.

For the second time we tried out the Los Angeles group by sending an uncle of mine, José López, to pursuade them to support us. His mission had no better results than mine because Avila remained firm in his views.

About this time, a vessel arrived at San Diego from Monterey carrying Don Abel Stearns[51] who had been

[50] José María Avila, was a native of Sinaloa, who came to Los Angeles as a boy. His parents were Cornelio Avila and Isabel Urquides. In manhood he became wealthy and in 1825 was chosen alcalde of Los Angeles. On December 5, 1831, Avila died in the first Battle of Cahuenga Pass. Governor Victoria was also wounded, and as a result of battle, he was forced to leave Alta California.

[51] Abel Stearns was a native of Massachusetts who lived in Mexico for three years and became a naturalized Mexican in 1828. He came to Alta California the following year, arriving at Monterey in July 1829. He came with the intention of obtaining a large tract of land, to be selected in the Sacramento-San Joaquín Basin. This was apparently in payment of a claim the Mexican government had promised him. During his negotiation for this grant he seemed to have incited the animosity of Governor Victoria. As a conse-

banished by Victoria. This gentleman, once ashore, told us that two days before, the general had left Monterey for the south with the intention of having Bandini and me hung because he believed we were disturbing the public peace. With this news, we hastened our arrangements and we invited Stearns himself to join us, which he agreed to do.

Finally, we agreed to set the date of the revolt for the 30th of November 1831. This agreement was reached about eight or nine o'clock at night. For that purpose, fifteen of us citizens gathered together, namely: Ignacio López, José López, Juan López, Juan María Marron, Andrés Ibarra, Antonio Ibarra, Damaso Alipaz, Gervacio Alipaz, Abel Stearns, Juan Osuna, Silverio Ríos, and some one else (whose name I don't remember) besides Carrillo, Bandini, myself and a Mexican *cholo*,[52] who was the one that carried the ammunition – his name I don't recall either. We started the march toward the cavalry barracks, surprised the guard and took all the arms. It was Señor Carrillo who overpowered the sentry and took away his firearm.

It was agreed that I should be the one to apprehend Captain Don Santiago Argüello,[53] company com-

quence of Victoria's feelings, Stearns was banished, but returned to take an active part in the leadership of the revolt in 1831. Don Abel, as a Los Angeles resident, figured prominently in California events until his death at San Francisco in 1871.

52 Cholo: very much a nobody; peasant type.

53 Santiago Argüello was a native of California, born at Monterey, 1791. He became a cadet in the San Francisco Company at fourteen and was promoted to captain in 1831. Reluctantly he took part in the revolt against Victoria. He retired from active service in 1835, thereafter following a political career. In 1829 Argüello obtained the Tia Juana Rancho and in 1846 due to his friendliness to the American cause was given an honorary commission as captain in the California Battalion, and was also appointed a member of the legislative council in 1847. As a youth he married Pilar, daughter of Francisco Ortega of

mander, since I was in better relations with him, and so I did. Argüello was playing "tresilla" [54] with his wife, Doña Pilar Ortega and Ensign Don Ignacio del Valle. I entered with a gun in each hand and charged them to surrender, begging him at the same time to forgive the violence with which I presented myself in his house because the circumstances demanded it. I asked Argüello and Valle to go with me to the home of Captain Don Pablo de la Portilla, commander-at-arms.

Argüello agreed to go with me and only asked that I get rid of the two armed men who accompanied me. Shortly after, we three went to Portilla's house. When we got there, Argüello said to Portilla, "Here we are, Pico's prisoners!" Portilla answered, "I, too, am a prisoner of Señor Bandini." In effect this was so. Bandini had agreed to apprehend Portilla and had carried it out.

We all sat down to confer. Until the moment of their capture the two captains and the ensign had not the slightest suspicion of what we were contriving. In that conference Bandini presented the plan of revolt. The officials confessed that all the assertions in the plan of revolt were true and well founded. Bandini then presented considerations in order to pursuade them to join us, but this was not achieved. They pledged themselves, under protest, not to take any steps against us until the conclusion of the affair.

Bandini and I offered to set them free, taking upon

Santa Barbara. They had twenty-two children. Santiago was tall, stout, of fair complexion and black hair. His career was honorable though not brilliant. He died at his Tia Juana Ranch in 1862.

[54] Tresilla, also called "hombre": a card game of Spanish origin, played by three people. As there were four persons present, one must have been a spectator.

ourselves the responsibility of maintaining peace and order. From there we went to the barracks, and we decided to go and take the artillery pieces which were in the charge of three or four artillerymen, and this we did without any difficulty and we took the pieces to the barracks.

That same night, the corporal and four soldiers, who formed the barrack's guard, joined our side.

The following day, December 1, 1831, we sent that same corporal and the four soldiers ahead to patrol San Mateo Point [55] to prevent any person passing through to Los Angeles. They stayed there on detail for eight to ten days.

Next, Bandini and I busied ourselves again trying to pursuade the officials to join us. This lasted several days until, at last, after they had various military conferences, they decided to espouse our cause, with the understanding that Commander-General Echeandía, who was in San Diego, be put in charge of and direct the campaign against Victoria. The same day in which they joined us, the officers asked us how we had dared revolt, being so small in number. We answered them that if it were true we were going to uprise with only twelve men, knowing that in the barracks were around thirty cavalrymen (as many in the squadron from Mazatlán) besides the artillerymen, in taking that step, we had also counted on the help of everyone in the country – that we had arranged on the 30th of November that the towns of all the territory would revolt, which was not the truth. Besides, we gave them to understand that we had agreed – all Mexicans who should refuse to cooperate

55 San Mateo Point is a coastal point in San Diego County about two miles south of the town of San Clemente and just across the Orange County line.

with us against Victoria would be expelled from the country as soon as we were victorious.

Immediately after, the officers demanded Echeandía be named chief. Bandini left in search of him and in a few moments returned, accompanied by him. Echeandía took the chair as president of the junta, and manifested his consent to the desires of the officials. Having accepted the command, we rebels placed ourselves under his orders.

The officials signed the pronunciamiento.[56] That same day or the next, Captain Argüello collected his troops and Captain Portilla did the same with the Mazatecos, letting them know that they had joined the uprising and then the soldiers did the same. From that moment on, Echeandía began to give commands, relieving us of responsibility in the matter.

Two or three days later, a group of fifty men under the command of Captain Don Pablo de la Portilla left for Los Angeles, Don José Carrillo accompanying them. The force was probably ten leagues from Los Angeles when Señor Victoria arrived at San Fernando, about five o'clock in the afternoon. He brought with him Captain Romualdo Pacheco,[57] Ensign Rodrigo del Pliego and a detachment of about twenty-seven soldiers.

---

[56] Pronunciamiento: insurrection or a declaration on insurrection.

[57] Romualdo Pacheco, a native of Guanajuato, Mexico, was a sub-lieutenant of engineers who came to Alta California in 1825 with Governor Echeandía, as his aide-de-camp. In his capacity as army engineer he guided survey expeditions as far east as the Colorado River and up the coast to Fort Ross. In 1827 and '28 he was acting commandant at Monterey. He became a lieutenant in 1829 shortly after taking charge of the garrison at Santa Barbara. In 1831 he was granted the use of a portion of Rancho Simi. His untimely death at the Cahuenga battle site in December 1831 was a definite loss to California history. This fine man left a wife of only two years and two infant sons, one but a month old. His widow, Ramona, was the daughter of Joaquín Carrillo of San Diego.

Victoria asked Father Francisco Ibarra[58] if he had
word of an uprising in San Diego. The father replied
that nothing was known there about such a revolt. Victoria then produced some three or four letters that
Carrillo, Bandini and I had sent to Santa Barbara to
Don Carlos, Don Anastasio, and Don Domingo Carrillo,[59] informing them that the officers and troops of

[58] Francisco González de Ibarra was a native of Viana, Spain, born in
1782. A Franciscan padre who came to Mexico in 1819 and on to California
the following year. After a short visit to Mission San Luis Obispo he received
the administrative job at San Fernando. Here he served for fifteen years, in
1835 retiring to Mexico. He returned within a year, serving the last three
years of his life at San Luis Rey. Father Ibarra died there of a stroke in 1842.
He was a good manager, and adversely, was known for his boasting. He
boasted his mission accomplishments were much more than that of other
padres. His bragging and certain criticisms of authority prompted the nickname "Padre Napoleón."

[59] Don Carlos, Don Anastasio, and Don Domingo Carrillo were sons of
José Raimundo Carrillo. (See note 41 for Domingo.) Anastasio was born at
Santa Barbara in 1788 and became a sergeant in the Santa Barbara Company,
distinguishing himself as an Indian fighter, and retiring from the army in
1836 with full pay. He married Concepción García and this union produced
seven children. Anastasio served as mayordomo of San Fernando Mission in
1837 and was grantee of Rancho Punta de la Concepción that same year. In
1845 he also received a grant of Rancho Cieneguitas. In his later years he
remained a prominent citizen of Santa Barbara.

Carlos Antonio de Jesús Carrillo was also born at Santa Barbara, five years
earlier in 1783. He became a soldier in the Monterey Company when a boy of
fifteen. Carlos made a fine name for himself and was sergeant of the Santa
Barbara Company from 1811 to about 1825. He became a member of the
diputación in 1828 after having left the military the previous year. Carlos
spent the years 1830-31 in Mexico as a member of Congress. He was a serious,
earnest politician having been inspired by Captain de la Guerra; he worked
particularly in favor of the missions. One of his speeches became the first
essay of a native Californian to be printed as a book. Back in California, he
was granted Rancho Sespé in 1833. He continued in the political field and was
a warm supporter of Alvarado in 1836. The following year he received an
appointment from Mexico City, to be governor of California. He made his
capital in Los Angeles and for two years functioned ineffectually, mainly because Alvarado whom he had so faithfully supported in 1836, would not give
up his total interest in the governorship. In 1845 he was the grantee of Santa
Rosa Island. As he was a popular man, his poor showing as a politician was
due to a lack of aggressiveness. Carrillo died in 1852, at the age of 69.

San Diego had joined us and inviting them to do the
same. But when they received the letters, Victoria had
already passed Santa Barbara. The three brothers
had gone to consult with old Captain Don José de la
Guerra,[60] and he had advised them to send the letters
to Victoria, the very ones he, Victoria, received before
arriving at San Fernando. I must not forget to say that
Domingo Carrillo had been left as commander upon
the departure of Captain Pacheco with Victoria.

[60] José de la Guerra y Noriega. A native of Spain, born March 6, 1779 to
Juan José and wife María Teresa de Noriega. When a young man he spent
three years in Mexico, clerking for a merchant uncle, Pedro Noriega. To his
uncle's disappointment, he enrolled in 1798 in the San Diego Company, as a
cadet. His unit came to California in 1801. In 1804 Second Lieutenant José de
la Guerra obtained his king's permission to marry Antonia, daughter of Raimundo Carrillo. Within two more years he was promoted to lieutenant of the
Santa Barbara Company, shortly thereafter he was transferred to San Diego.
In 1808, his uncle Pedro having forgiven his indiscretion and poor judgement
in joining the army, began sending José large consignments of goods, the sale
of which greatly improved his financial position. In 1810 he was sent on a
military assignment to Mexico City, but was arrested in San Blas by insurgents and forced to return to California. Most of the remainder of his military
career was spent at Santa Barbara. He was promoted to captain in 1818. In
1821-22 he was busy obtaining ranchos, the grant of Rancho Conejo causing
him to quarrel with the local padres. Trying for the governorship in 1822, he
failed due to his Spanish birth. His political career was not as successful as
was his military and business activities. In 1830 he purchased a cargo schooner
and evidently had another built, the one being inadequate to handle his grow-
ing import trade. José de la Guerra did not join the movement against Victoria
in 1831, but became an active supporter of Alvarado's cause in 1836. For his
loyalty, Alvarado granted him the Rancho National in the Salinas area. After
serving fifty-two years in the army, he asked for retirement in 1840; in the
meantime, he had been unable to collect much of his back pay because of
unrests in California during the previous decade. He retired in 1842 short
some $12,000 due him. José was never friendly to the United States but gen-
erally remained quiet about his sentiments. He died in Santa Barbara in 1858,
a wealthy man. He left one hundred direct descendants; his sons soon
spent his fortune. A man of integrity, a bit prone to quarreling as a young
man; his judgement was good; his leanings conservative. He was always
popular and in the later years of his life he was considered the patriarch of
his beloved Santa Barbara.

When Victoria placed these letters before Father Ibarra, the father advised him to set off for Los Angeles without delay. Victoria replied that it appeared best to send the majordomo[61] of the mission to Los Angeles to inquire of the alcalde what was known for certain about the revolution. The majordomo came with a letter from Victoria to the alcalde asking information. He arrived at dusk, handed the letter to Alcalde Vicente Sánchez, and the alcalde answered that there was not the slightest rumor of a revolution – that all was peaceful. At about eight or nine o'clock that same night, our force of fifty men arrived at Los Angeles and seized the alcalde. At that time a brother of his, named Juan Sánchez, was at the house. He disguised himself with a dress of the alcalde's wife and covered his head with a shawl. Thus disguised, he left the house passing our force, who did not suspect it was not a woman. Juan Sánchez took a horse and went to the jefe político, whom he notified of what had occurred.

Alcalde Sánchez was placed in fetters and conducted to the guardhouse. All the prisoners who were in jail were set at liberty and took part in the revolution.

The next day, Portilla left with a force and encamped in the low hills of Los Angeles in the direction of Cahuenga.[62]

About ten or eleven a.m., Victoria approached with

---

61 Mayordomo (majordomo) is one who manages a rancho.

62 Cahuenga: a pass in the hills; a name possibly derived from a Gabrielino Indian ranchería located in the area. Traveling northwest, one leaves the coastal slope in Hollywood and traverses this pass to the San Fernando Valley. Two battles were fought in the pass during the Mexican period; and it was at a small ranch house, not far from the north entrance to the pass, where the *Californios* signed a treaty with Fremont on January 13, 1847, ending the Mexican War in California.

his force. He drew near the force of Don Pablo. At some distance, Victoria asked Portilla to come to his side and abandon the troops under his command. At this, José Antonio Carrillo said to Portilla, "If you take one step forward I will give the command to fire!" Victoria drew still nearer. Captain Pacheco (as we later learned through one of his own soldiers who was later wounded, José María Avila) pointed out to him the folly of pretending to attack a force as superior as Portilla's, which was some one hundred men. Victoria replied: "He who wears skirts should not follow me." These words provoked Pacheco who said he was not ruled by skirts. He took out his sword and ordered his troops to march onward. He swung his sword at José Antonio Carrillo, who stood next to Portilla, with José María Avila at his other side.

Carrillo warded off the blow with his gun and Avila took a pistol from his pocket and shot Pacheco, who fell dead as the bullet passed through his heart. Avila then threw down the pistol and flourishing a spear, went among the enemy asking, who was the general, as it was him he sought. He found Victoria and saying, "You black bastard, I have been looking for you." He gave him a blow on the side with his lance. At that moment, Avila's horse moved back. He intended to lunge at Victoria again when he received a shot from a soldier named Leandro Morales, from Mazatlán. Avila fell near Victoria. Victoria then got up and with his sabre was about to kill Avila. Avila, nevertheless succeeded in grasping him and throwing him to the ground. Just then, a corporal of Victoria's forces, Guerrero by name, drew near, intending to kill Avila. Avila took a pistol, he had concealed in his boot and with it wounded Guerrero in the foot. Guerrero fell to the ground.

At this stage of the fight Tomás Talamantes,[63] one of our men, came up and while still mounted, addressed a blow to Victoria but only succeeded in scratching his cheek with the end of the sabre, because the other moved his body over. This ended the battle with Victoria withdrawing. Portilla and his men had already left, leaving the field of battle to Victoria.

I had forgotten to say that the soldier, Leandro Morales, and a civilian named José Pérez, shot at each other, but as the guns failed to go off, they started fighting with the butts of those same guns until another man approached. Morales withdrew and Pérez did likewise.

Victoria went to San Gabriel with his people and Portilla encamped at Nietos Ranch [64] with his.

PICO'S FIRST GOVERNORSHIP

The next day Victoria sent a letter to Portilla advising him that he surrendered. This, in truth, was the best thing left to do because he was extremely unpopular due to his severity and despotism, and he had no followers; besides, he was wounded and incapable of carrying on the campaign. Portilla at once informed Commander-General Echeandía, who was now very near

---

63 Tomás Talamantes is possibly the brother of Felipe Talamantes, who was the grantee of Rancho La Ballona in 1839.

64 Rancho Los Nietos was one of the three earliest grants in California sharing that honor with Rancho San Rafael and Rancho San Pedro. Los Nietos was granted to Manuel Nieto in 1784 only three years after the founding of the Pueblo de Los Angeles. The original grant included all the land from the San Gabriel River to the Santa Ana River and from the San Gabriel mountains to the sea. The rancho was later divided into five parts to accommodate Nieto's heirs. Thus were created the Ranchos Santa Gertrudis, Los Coyotes, Los Cerritos, Los Alamitos, and Las Bolsas.

the Nietos Ranch. There, Echeandía stopped and we had a drink in honor of the triumph of our cause. We came directly to Los Angeles, where we decided Victoria's fate, ordering him shipped from San Diego, to the interior of the Republic of Mexico. Our cause, then, was triumphant and we busied ourselves in organizing the government and deciding to whom should be assigned the posts of jefe político and comandante-general. While this was going on, there arrived from the north, Señores Mariano G. Vallejo,[65] Juan Bautista

[65] Mariano Guadalupe Vallejo was born in Monterey on July 7, 1808. His parents were Ignacio Vallejo and María de Lugo. The story goes that Ignacio assisted at the birth of Francisca Carrillo (daughter of Joaquín Carrillo) his future bride and was betrothed to her from that time. They were married when she was fourteen. Vallejo entered the military as a cadet of the Monterey Company in 1824. In 1838 he was made comandante-general of California with a permanent rank of lieutenant-colonel of cavalry in May of 1842. The Americans honored him with a commission as colonel of cavalry in September 1846. Considering the lack of educational facilities during the Mexican period, Don Mariano was fortunate to have received the finest to be obtained. He was recipient of Rancho Petaluma in 1834. The following year he was instructed to lay out a pueblo at Solano Mission and was made director of colonization. This action was taken to counteract the pressure of the Russian encroachment at Fort Ross. Vallejo relations with the northern Indians were always of the best and through the years he proved to be an outstanding leader. By 1837 he was the foremost man in California and one of the wealthiest. His fine *casa* was on the plaza in Sonoma where he entertained in princely fashion. In the sectional strife of 1837-39 Vallejo took no military part, although he was an influential backer of Alvarado. Of all the Californians, he was perhaps most aware of the dangers of foreign conquest and did more than any other to prepare for such an event. When the Americans came as conquerors Mariano Vallejo declared friendship toward their cause; however, this did not deter his arrest and imprisonment by the Americans. In December 1846 he gave the land to found the town of Benicia. Originally the city was to be called Francisca in honor of his wife, but Robert Semple, in advertising the land, listed it as Benicia, another given name of Doña Vallejo. In 1849 Mariano was a member of the California Constitutional Convention at Monterey and the following year a member of the first state senate. The money he lost in the disastrous attempt to make Benicia the permanent state capital cost him the greater part of his fortune. Highly respected he spent most of his remaining life in Sonoma, where he died in 1890.

Alvarado,[66] and Antonio María Osio. [67] I do not remember if any more came. These gentlemen took an
interest in the organization of the government. As the
first or senior voting member, I proposed myself to
take the oath and assume the political leadership. For
the act of taking oath, it was necessary to have on hand,
the Book of the Gospels and other sacramental objects
of the church. The *Padre Ministro* (father minister)
refused to lend us the keys to the church so that they
could be taken out. Then, Juan Bautista Alvarado
crawled through a skylight, opened the door from the
inside and took out the necessary things.

The chamber, having convened, had a table with all
the necessary things placed at the door of the parish
church of Los Angeles. If my memory doesn't fail me,
Don Mariano G. Vallejo, who was, after me, the eldest
voting member, administered the customary oath; that
is, to uphold and obey the constitution and to discharge
legally the duties that were entrusted to me.

After I had taken the oath, Señor Echeandía, who
had been nearing Los Angeles, arrived on or about the
next day. He had left San Diego because of the counter-
revolution in Monterey that had been started by Don

66 Juan Bautista Alvarado, son of Sergeant José F. Alvarado and María
Josefa Vallejo, was born at Monterey, Feb. 14, 1809. While still in his teens,
he held the important position of secretary of the diputación, and thereafter
his career was largely political. He was the first native born governor of
California serving from December 1836 to July 1837. His administration was
somewhat less than commendable because of the interference of his alcoholic
tendencies. His excessive drinking on his wedding day resulted in a proxy
marriage to María Martina Castro; the bridegroom being represented by his
half-brother, José Antonio Estrada. Alvarado died on the San Pablo rancho
July 13, 1882.

67 Antonio María Osio, a native of Baja California, spent his adult years
in Alta California where he was active in important political positions, mainly
that of customs agent.

Agustín Vicente Zamorano,[68] the commanding captain of that town.

Echeandía expressed displeasure on learning that I had taken the oath as provisional jefe político and refused to recognize me as such. That disagreement was seconded by the ayuntamiento of Los Angeles but not by the people, notwithstanding that it may have been so recorded in the minutes of that body inasmuch as the people did not meet to give their opinion on this matter.

Various persons tried to persuade Alcalde Manuel Domínguez [69] to recognize me as jefe político but he refused, alleging as the sole reason that we had been reared together as boys, without remembering that I had recognized him as alcalde. Perhaps Señor Domínguez favored what Echeandía had said in an official letter to the deputation about my lack of ability to discharge such a thorny task.

In this state of affairs, news arrived in Los Angeles that Lieutenant Juan María Ibarra [70] was approaching

---

[68] Agustín Vicente Zamorano was born in Florida of Spanish parents, and entered the Mexican army as a cadet. In 1825, when an alférez (junior ofcer), he arrived in California with Governor Echeandía to serve as secretary. He married María Louisa Argüello in 1827. In 1832 Zamorano refused to accept the results of the revolt against Victoria; made a counter-revolt against Echeandía, and sustained himself as comandante general of the north until the arrival of Figueroa in 1833. From 1834 to 1836 he was captain of the Presidio of Monterey, and during this period operated the first printing shop in California. He died in 1842.

[69] Manuel Domínguez, born in 1803, had a long association with Rancho San Pedro. In 1827 he married María Engracia de Cota. He was active in public affairs, and eventually in 1832 was elected alcalde and judge of the first instance for the Pueblo of Los Angeles. Domínguez died in 1882.

[70] Juan María Ibarra, born in 1819, was a lieutenant in the escuadrón of Mazatlan (an escuadrón or squadron consisted of thirty infantrymen). In 1832 he was a prominent supporter of Zamorano; he commanded forces that marched south from Monterey against Echeandía in San Diego in 1832. In 1833, he commanded the northern forces in California, and continued to do so until 1836, when he returned to Mexico.

with a considerable force. On learning this, Echeandía
moved his camp from Los Angeles and retreated to San
Diego, leaving here with me the deputation and some
of the citizens who recognized me as their governor.

When Ibarra and his troops were in the neighbor-
hood of Los Angeles, we all left for San Diego. While
there, Señor Echeandía decided to acknowledge me as
jefe político, so as to undertake the campaign against
Lieutenant Ibarra, who was in Los Angeles with his
troops.

We set out from San Diego for that campaign. At
San Luis Rey there was a disagreement between Señor
Bandini and Echeandía, I do not know about what. We
deputies took advantage of the opportunity and started
the march on our own to join Captain Barroso [71] who
had arrived at the banks of the San Gabriel River with
fourteen soldiers from San Diego and some five hundred Indians, armed with arrows and spears.

The night we arrived at Santa Ana, that is, the Yorba
ranch,[72] a man from Los Angeles came to inform us
that the town was calling for the jefe político and the
deputation. We joined forces with Barroso on the banks
of the San Gabriel.

---

[71] Leonardo Díez Barroso arrived in 1830 in California as a lieutenant, and
while stationed at San Diego, was promoted to captain. He returned to Mexico
in 1836.

[72] Rancho Santiago de Santa Ana was granted to Antonio Yorba and his
father-in-law, Juan Pablo Grijalva, sometime before 1800. In 1810 Don Antonio and a nephew, Pablo Peralta, came into its possession. Its location in
what is now Orange County, was on the east bank of the Santa Ana River
from the ocean front at present day Newport Beach to the Santa Ana Canyon
as its north boundary. The towns of Santa Ana, Orange, and Tustin are presently within its borders. Bernardo, son of Antonio, was in possession of the
property at the time of Pico's visit. The Yorba Rancho is not to be confused
with the adjacent Rancho Cañada de Santa Ana north of the river, granted to
Don Bernardo August 1, 1834.

Next day, Barroso sent a message to Lieutenant Ibarra telling him to abandon the town of Los Angeles or otherwise be attacked by the force under his command. About ten a.m. the next day Echeandía arrived where we were. He brought about one hundred men and two pieces of artillery mounted on wooden carts. We immediately started our march toward Los Angeles, and upon our arrival discovered that Ibarra and his forces had retreated to the north. Echeandía remained in the town a few days and then returned to San Diego.

During this time the deputation occupied itself with nothing more than to carry on communications with Echeandía and some with Zamorano in Monterey, ignoring the office each was pretending to hold.

Echeandía remained in San Diego, giving out orders, obeyed by none but the military, since not even the ayuntamiento of Los Angeles recognized his having any civil authority.

GOVERNOR FIGUEROA'S YEARS

The country continued thus until the arrival of Brigadier-General Don José Figueroa,[73] with the double title of Jefe Supremo Político and Comandante-General Inspector, at the end of 1832 or the beginning of 1833. As soon as Figueroa assumed his post, he sent circulars to the military and civilian authorities and issued a decree of pardon to all those who had taken part in the revolution against Victoria, calling at the same time on the officials to return and discharge their military obligations. Figueroa also sent officials to each

---

[73] José Figueroa, Mexican brigadier general, came to California in 1833, and ruled California as both political head and military leader until his death, Sept. 29, 1835. These two years are characterized as an era of tranquility.

one of the deputies to make known to them the pardon
that the supreme government had granted them.

I do not know what the others may have answered,
but for my part, I made it known to Figueroa that there
was no necessity for amnesty because after Victoria had
abandoned the country, I had done nothing more than
comply with the law in assuming the burden of political
leadership and that I would promptly answer any
charges the government would wish to make against
me. I did not receive a reply from the general, who
dedicated himself wholly to bringing peace to the country, which had subsisted nearly a year in complete
anarchy. Figueroa gained his objective and nothing
occurred to disturb the peace and order until the arrival
of the colony of Híjar and Padrés.[74]

As soon as Figueroa took charge, he convened the
deputation and always maintained cordial relations
with it, trying extremely hard to better the country's
situation in all its branches. Everything was progressing
well; the administration of justice had become a reality
and crimes and transgressions diminished noticeably.
With the tranquility that was established, business improved and public instruction was developed. It can be
said with certainty that the country was progressing
with a firm pace toward its well-being.

Don José María Híjar and Lieutenant Colonel Don
José María Padrés, adjutant-inspector of the troops,
arrived with a large colony, part of which disembarked

---

74 José María Padrés and José María Híjar were commissioned by Mexico
City to bring families to California and form a buffer colony against further
Russian encroachment. Two hundred and four colonists settled in Sonoma
Valley. Padrés and Híjar participated in a rebellion against Figueroa; each
were arrested and deported to Mexico.

in San Diego with Señor Híjar and the other part at Monterey with Señor Padrés.

Señor Híjar came with the double duties of jefe político and director of colonization. Much before taking political charge, Señor Figueroa had received a dispatch from the supreme government ordering him not to turn over the leadership to Híjar. This message was brought by special messenger who made the trip from Mexico by land in just a few days, and I later learned upon his return he died as a result of the exertions he suffered.

Señor Figueroa did not turn over the government to Híjar. The deputation, of which I was first vocal, was convened. I was at my ranch twelve leagues from San Diego when I received the notice and I started out immediately. The same day I left the ranch I arrived in Los Angeles, having traveled nearly sixty leagues using six horses. Next day, in Santa Barbara, I caught up with the rest of the deputies and we continued together to Monterey.

Several times I made the trip from San Diego to Los Angeles in one day with the sole object being to fight bulls the next day, which was our favorite sport.

Having arrived in Monterey, the deputation was installed presided over by the jefe político, Señor Figueroa, who made known that in consequence of having received a communication from the supreme government which he wished to place before the Chamber, he had called it together to advise him and to proceed according to its decisions. Figueroa's address having concluded, I recommended that he vacate the chair by virtue of the fact that what we were going to discuss pertained to his person. He left immediately and gave me the chair.

We read the communication referred to, and we were of the opinion that Señor Figueroa should not turn over the political command because that was what the supreme government had ordered, but that Señor Híjar should be recognized as director of colonization and the government should give him all the aid necessary to carry forward that undertaking.

Communications between Figueroa and Híjar continued with the result that the general named a commission from the group of deputies to settle the question as to whether the director of colonization should have in his charge the property of the missions, as he contended. The commission occupied itself with this subject and gave its judgement in opposition to the claims of Híjar. I will not concern myself further with this subject because Figueroa's manifesto contains all that occurred.

After everything was settled, the deputation adjourned.

Some months later (at the beginning of the year 1835), I being in Los Angeles, there was an uprising of Sonorans against General Figueroa led by Juan Gallardo,[75] also a Sonoran. This Gallardo appeared as chief, but the leaders of the movement were Guadalupe Apalátegui[76] (a Spaniard) and the physician, Torres.[77]

---

[75] Juan Gallardo was a shoemaker, and was a co-leader of fifty Sonorans who attempted in March 1835 to overthrow the government of California. The revolt failed.

[76] Guadalupe Apalátegui (Bancroft lists his surname as Antonio) was a co-leader in the Los Angeles revolt in 1835 against Governor Figueroa. He was arrested and deported to Mexico.

They revolted one day at dawn and seized the guard. They took possession of a small cannon belonging to the town and fired one shot. The alcalde, Francisco Javier Alvarado[78] (my brother-in-law, at whose house I was staying), went out. I accompanied him to the courthouse where I talked with Juan Gallardo and he let me know that he and his men had risen in revolt against Figueroa's government. Mounted on horseback, he produced the document containing the pronouncement and asked me to place it in the hands of the alcalde. The alcalde, noting its contents, called together the ayuntamiento to discuss the matter.

When the ayuntamiento was convened, I met Apalátegui on the street and advised him to go to the ayuntamiento to answer the objections that would be presented as it appeared to me that the plan was absurd. Among other things, they demanded that Captain Pablo de la Portilla remain in political and military command. Then I approached Gallardo, who was a person I esteemed, and told him of the necessity of disavowing it because the plan I had seen was impossible to put into effect:

1. Because they asked that Portilla be put in supreme political and military authority – a thing no one would accept.
2. Because, to begin the campaign against Monterey, it was necessary to attack all the privately owned places on the way – which would bring upon them general disapproval.

[77] Francisco Torres was a Mexican physician who came to California with the Padrés-Híjar colony. He was exiled in 1835 for participating in the Gallardo-Apalátegui revolt.

[78] Francisco Javier Alvarado, born in 1807, was a lifelong resident of Los Angeles. On May 24, 1829, he became Pío Pico's brother-in-law by marriage to María Tomasa Pico (see footnote 82).

Gallardo answered that Apalátegui and Torres had offered him a sum of money sufficient for the needs of the campaign. "But," he told me, "if by three this afternoon they have not given me $4000 or $5000, Torres and Apalátegui will be turned over to the alcalde and I will disperse the force." That is exactly what happened. About three or four o'clock that afternoon, he brought those two individuals to the alcalde and the alcalde put each one in a pair of fetters and put them in prison under the guard of civilians. The alcalde promptly issued a call to the residents and several presented themselves, among them Don Manuel Requeña [79] and Don Antonio María Lugo,[80] Don Vicente Sánchez, Don Manuel Domínguez, and other notables. The civilians took custody of the prisoners and I was named their commander.

Gallardo, after turning in Apalátegui and Torres, had his men disarm themselves and return to their homes. That was the end of the tumult caused by the Sonorans.

I had given Gallardo a guarantee that nothing would happen to him if he did what we asked, therefore he was not molested, and when General Figueroa came, he called him and tolerantly advised him not to become involved in matters of this nature again – saying at the same time to Gallardo, "Remember, in Sonora I pardoned you for the same kind of act." This same

[79] Manuel Requeña, a native of Yucatán, came to California in 1834, and remained a respected citizen. He is remembered as the public prosecutor at the Apalátegui trial.

[80] Antonio María Lugo was born in 1775. In early life he was a soldier; later a wealthy and widely known rancher. He involved himself in public affairs, including the American period, until his death in 1860.

Gallardo had been married two times in California but he and his wives died without offspring.

The delivery of Apalátegui and Torres occurred about sunset. The men offered to go after their arms and by eight o'clock that night none of them had returned. Beforehand, I had told the alcalde and the rest that it appeared to me to be more convenient to convey the prisoners to San Gabriel where Lieutenant Colonel Don Nicolás Gutiérrez [81] was commander, with a force of some fifty men. But the majority of the men were of the opinion that it would be shameful to the town, if it should be said that we could not take care of two prisoners. So it was decided they should remain in Los Angeles.

The alcalde, seeing that by eight o'clock the men had not returned, asked me what should be done and I repeated that they should be taken to San Gabriel. Then he asked me if I minded conducting them and I acceded to it. I called together a few friends, whom I trusted and that same night about eleven o'clock the prisoners were in the custody of the military commander. Before leaving Los Angeles, I had the fetters removed from the prisoners and had them mount horses. I went ahead with three men. A little further back came the prisoners

---

[81] Nicolás Gutiérrez came to California as a captain with Governor Figueroa in 1833, and was promoted that year to lieutenant colonel. In 1835 he was elevated to the rank of comandante general, and it was during this period that Los Angeles was designated capital of Alta California. He held this office on two occasions, and during 1836 he was also *jefe político*. The secularization of San Gabriel Mission in 1834-1836, proceeded under his office of *Comisionado*. When Mariano Chico, a Mexican appointed governor of California, was ousted, Gutiérrez became head of the provisional government and he in turn was overthrown by Juan Bautista Alvarado. Following this, Gutiérrez returned to Mexico. Bancroft states that Gutiérrez was "an easy going, faithful officer of ordinary abilities and of not very strict morals."

between two men armed with lances. Four more men
marched as the rear guard. They had orders, that if
they heard a shot either in front or in back of them, they
were to kill the prisoners. I will admit that the order
was rash because anyone could have fired a shot and the
prisoners would have perished. So when they were returned from San Gabriel to Los Angeles a few days
later, they begged Commander Gutiérrez not to place
them in my charge.

Since nothing new transpired, in a few days I returned to my home in San Diego.

I was married in 1834 in the month of February and
General Figueroa was my best man. The wedding took
place on the 24th in Los Angeles. My wife was María
Ignacia Alvarado, daughter of Javier Alvarado and
María Ignacia Amador.[82] After the wedding, I accompanied the general to Santa Barbara, where we arrived
the 18th of March. There, on the 19th, we celebrated
Figueroa's birthday. We had a grand party – high mass
was sung, musketry salutes, bull-fighting, and a grand
ball. The 21st, I returned to Los Angeles, taking the
road with the general and his officers as far as Carpen-
tería.[83] There, officers Nicolás Gutiérrez, Domingo

---

[82] Francisco Javier Alvarado was a career soldier, with the rank of sergeant. He served mainly in the Los Angeles area. In 1788 he married María
Ignacia, daughter of Pedro Amador. Their son, also named Francisco Javier
married Pío Pico's sister, and their daughter María Ignacia married Pío Pico
in 1834. The county of Amador is the only county in California named after
a Mexican family, specifically, Sergeant Pedro Amador, or his son José María,
or possibly both.

[83] Carpintería is a seaside town thirteen miles east of Santa Barbara, which
existed as an Indian village long before the first Spanish explorers arrived
at the site. Father Juan Crespi was the chronicler for the Portolá expedition
in 1769. On August 17 of that year Father Crespi writes, "The Indians have
many canoes, and at the time were building one, for which reason the soldiers

Carrillo and Capt. Navarrete[84] sought permission to accompany me to San Buenaventura. But, taking advantage of the general's generosity, they came as far as Los Angeles, staying here three or four days.

At the time of the disturbance by Apalátegui, Torres, Gallardo, etc., General Figueroa came to Los Angeles, as I said before. From here he went to San Diego (in April) and named me administrator of the Mission of San Luis Rey and I was in charge of its administration until 1840, at which time Governor Alvarado took it away from me.

The general returned to Monterey and passed away there in September or October.

Figueroa was short of stature, plump, dark skinned, beardless, and about fifty years old. A very refined and amiable man. His administration was very honest and all classes respected and loved him. His death, therefore, was deeply felt throughout the country.

POLITICAL TURMOIL, 1836-1840

Figueroa was succeeded by Don José Castro[85] as

named the town La Carpintería (the carpenter shop), while I christened it with the name of San Roque." Nearby the village are asphalt pits which were used by the Indian boat-builders from ancient time.

[84] Bernardo Navarrete was a Mexican lieutenant in the Monterey Company. (The rank of lieutenant is according to Bancroft.) He arrived in California in January 1833 on the "Catalina" in company with General José Figueroa, and Nicolás Gutiérrez, and remained until that time Gutiérrez found it necessary to return to Mexico.

[85] José Castro, son of José Tiburcio, was born about 1810, and early records of him are confusing as it is difficult to distinguish between father and son, both generally called José. Being a rebel at heart, his career was a most stormy one, as indicated by over a page of references in fine print in Bancroft's *Pioneer Register*. In 1860 he was killed in a drunken brawl in Baja California while serving as a military commander on the frontier. Bancroft comments: "He was not a very able man, but with ten times his ability and resources no resistance could have been offered to the U.S.; he was not a very

political chief and Lieutenant Colonel Gutiérrez as commandant-general.

Don José Castro succeeded as political chief by virture of the refusal of Don José Antonio Estudillo,[86] who was the senior vocal, to assume that charge, feigning as an excuse that he was sick. It is to be noted that when General Figueroa found himself gravely ill, he sought Señor Estudillo so that he would prepare himself to take possession of the leadership. Señor Castro held this position a very short time and then turned it over to Commandant-General Gutiérrez, I do not remember for what reason.

Several months later in that same year of 1836, Colonel Don Mariano Chico [87] came to California with the double title of civil and military governor, lasting but a short time in that office. I never knew him nor do I

brave man, but he showed no cowardice in the operations of '46. Indeed, his record as a public man in Upper California was, on the whole, not a bad one. He had much energy, was popular with most classes, was true to his friends, and as a public officer fairly honest. About his private character there is great difference of opinion among competent witnesses, native and foreign, who knew him well. He must have had some good qualities, yet it is clear that he had some very bad ones. He was addicted to many vices, and when drunk, especially in his later years, was rough to the verge of brutality; yet a kind-hearted man when sober. Of commonplace abilities and education, in most respects inferior to such men as Vallejo, Bandini, Alvarado and Carrillo. . ."

86 José Antonio Estudillo, son of José María Estudillo was born in 1805. During the Mexican period he was active in various public capacities, mainly in the San Diego area. Under United States rule he served as San Diego's treasurer and county assessor. He died in 1852. Bancroft states: "A man of excellent character, of good education for his time and country, and of wide influence in the south."

87 Mariano Chico arrived in California in 1836 to take over the governorship. He lasted three months, during which time he made himself the most hated ruler the province ever had. The climax came when he appeared in the place of honor at a public function, accompanied by his mistress, whom he endeavored to pass off as his niece, and who was at the time under arrest for adultery. The uproar over the incident was so great that Chico took refuge aboard a ship, that shortly later carried him to Mexico.

remember receiving any messages from him even though I was administering the Mission of San Luis Rey which was dependent upon the government. I knew nothing of his character, only that it was said that he was a crude man, very extravagant, with pretensions of being a poet, physician, etc. When he left for Mexico, he said he would return with sufficient forces to have his authority respected. In his place was left the same Lieutenant Colonel Gutiérrez. A very few days after he took command, at the end of 1836, the inhabitants of Monterey rebelled against him under the leadership of Juan Bautista Alvarado and José Castro, who later got Mariano Guadelupe Vallejo to join them. The actual leader of the revolution, it was said, was the customshouse inspector, Don Angel Ramirez.[88] The revolution in the north succeeded and Señor Gutiérrez and several of his officers were exiled from the country as well as the district judge, Don Luis del Castillo Negrete,[89] who sailed from San Diego.

[88] Angel Ramírez was an ex-friar and revolutionist who came overland from Tepic in 1834 with an appointment as administrator of the Monterey customshouse; he came largely because the government in Mexico wished to rid themselves of him. He appears to have been a scheming trouble-maker all his life, and it is said by his contemporaries, "had he been president he would have conspired against himself." He conspired against Governor Alvarado in 1837, and was accordingly arrested for his complicity to incite Indians to aid in the revolt; thereafter he was compelled to live out his life under surveillance in the missions. He died in 1840 at San Luis Obispo, a victim of syphillis.

[89] Luis del Castillo Negrete was a Spaniard, his father having been an attorney of the Council of the Indies. He was educated at Alcalá, Toledo and Granada in philosophy, mathematics, and law, and thereafter, in 1820, he left Spain. Negrete arrived in Monterey in September 1834 with an appointment of district judge of California. He also acted as legal advisor to Governor Gutiérrez. He was a bitter opponent of Governor Alvarado who succeeded Gutiérrez; he returned to Mexico voluntarily with Governor Gutiérrez. Thereafter he served as governor of Baja California and died in 1843. Bancroft rated him as "a very able lawyer, and a brilliant, accomplished gentleman."

We learned that Alvarado and Castro had rebelled with a plan already formulated, declaring this territory free and sovereign and refusing obedience to the supreme government.

Alvarado and Castro came down with a force because the south did not want to accept their plan nor recognize Alvarado as governor. I was in Los Angeles when they drew near and I was commissioned (in company with the alcalde, Don José Sepúlveda) to have an interview with those northern leaders. We held the interview at the San Fernando Mission where I invited Alvarado to join me in one of the orchards of that establishment where we could talk. There I made plain to him the difficulties involved in carrying out the pronouncement. The result of our long conversation was: to recognize the general government; not to expel a single Mexican against whom there did not appear legal cause; and that any person who was a Mexican citizen could hold any public office, if he had the intelligence necessary to do so. Under these conditions I offered him my cooperation, so that he could be recognized as governor. At the same time, I offered to go to Los Angeles without the necessity of an armed force so that he could establish contact with the authorities. Alvarado came to the city (having come to an agreement with me and accepted my propositions) with a small escort. I did not accompany him. Sepúlveda and I went to the ayuntamiento to give an account of our mission. I was not present at any of the conferences that took place afterwards between Alvarado and the ayuntamiento but I learned in a manner worthy of belief that he offered the ayuntamiento the same he had promised me – that is, modification of the pronouncement as regards the necessity of formal recognition of the supreme government and the existing general laws of the nation.

The ayuntamiento was in accord to recognize Alvarado as governor. He left for Santa Barbara where he returned to support of the original pronouncement, declaring California a free and sovereign state, that would not recognize the supreme government of Mexico, until the federal system should be reestablished there under the constitution of 1824.

Los Angeles and San Diego again refused to recognize that arrangement. We continued not to recognize it. Alvarado and Castro came back to San Gabriel with considerable forces.

I remember that Don Juan Rocha [90] was administrator of San Gabriel and had been called here to aid the ayuntamiento in keeping order and preventing disturbances, such as had occurred at Monterey and other places to the north.

Señor Rocha told me one time in a conversation, that he was in charge of an armed force he had organized in Los Angeles and that he had marched with it to San Fernando to prevent the entrance of the northerners into Los Angeles. When the opposing forces came almost in view of each other, Don José Sepúlveda [91] and

[90] Juan José Rocha came to California with Echeandía in 1825, as a brevet alférez. It appears his coming to California was a two-year sentence of banishment. For a period Rocha commanded the Monterey detachment of the San Blas Company. In later years his name appears frequently in official records, partly due to his activities as acting commander of the southern forces in the sectional war of 1837, and because of his terms as administrator for the secularization of San Gabriel and San Juan Capistrano missions. He died in San Diego at a date not recorded.

[91] For José Sepúlveda, Bancroft does not offer an historical sketch. However, he is mentioned as a regidor (alderman) of Los Angeles in 1833-34, and he was active in political affairs, and is credited as taking a prominent part

others who had accompanied him, approached the
northern forces and conferred with their chiefs, with
the result that hostilities did not break out. On this
occasion I was at San Luis Rey and did not know what
was going on.

After these occurrences, Don Carlos Antonio Carrillo received his appointment as governor. With this
appointment, he was given the authority to establish the
capital in any place the circumstances of the country
permitted, and he chose Los Angeles. Perhaps basing
himself on the fact that already there existed a supreme
decree giving Los Angeles the status of city and capital of the territory. Here he took his oath before the
ayuntamiento, presided by Alcalde Gil Ibarra.[92]

Shortly afterwards, Governor Carrillo was faced
with difficulties in having his authority respected, be-

---

on both sides of the sectional quarrels between the north and south. In 1842
eleven leagues, located in present Orange County, were granted to him. He
died in Sonora in 1875. Regarding the quarrel between the north and south,
Robert Cameron Gillingham, writing in *The Rancho San Pedro,* states, "The
period from 1836 through 1838 was marked by considerable military and political conflict in the Mexican government of California . . . centered
principally in the capital of Monterey, but threatened to bring open warfare
to southern California. Early in January, 1837, the ayuntamiento of Los Angeles appointed José Sepúlveda and Manuel Dominguez to represent the
pueblo at a special conference with Governor Alvarado. . . The purpose
of the meeting was to dissuade the governor from making an attack on the
Los Angeles area, and at the same time to ascertain the extent of military
forces under his command. When Governor Alvarado was informed of the
grievances at issue, and that local authorities in the south were prepared to
resist, he decided to return to Monterey and await the settlement of disputes,
principally over land grants, by higher officials in Mexico."

[92] Gil Ibarra was born in San Diego in 1784. The records show he was
síndico (city attorney) of Los Angeles in 1831, and later in 1836-37 the alcalde. He was prominent as a partisan of the southern faction against Alvarado in 1837-38, and on several occasions was arrested by northern military
forces. In 1841, the Rancho Rincon de la Brea (in present Orange County) of
one league (4,453 acres) was granted to him.

cause Señor Alvarado did not want to recognize him.
I was in San Luis Rey and I received a message from
Carrillo calling me to Los Angeles so that I could help
him raise funds. He had solicited certain sums from the
merchant Don Luis del Aliso (that was what everyone
called Señor de Vignes)[93] who had answered that he
would give them over my guarantee.

I went to Los Angeles and served the governor in
what he had asked of me. With the money he was
loaned, he commenced organizing a force to impose
respect, and managed to gather a considerable one of
over one hundred men under the command of Captain
Don Juan Castañeda.[94] This force left Los Angeles to
occupy Santa Barbara where there was a garrison that
recognized Señor Alvarado.

Captain Castañeda arrived at Cerrito del Voluntario
near Santa Barbara. There, Father President Narciso
Durán[95] and Captain José de la Guerra conferred with
Castañeda and agreed that he would not attack Santa
Barbara but would retire with his force to San Buenaventura. At the same time, the force from Santa Barbara
would remain there and in no event must go past the

[93] Jean Luis Vignes was born at Cadillac, France. He came to Monterey
from the Sandwich (Hawaiian) Islands and in 1831 moved to Los Angeles
and remained there until his death in 1863. To Vignes must go the credit for
being the first man in California to initiate the wine industry. The presence of
a large alder tree on his ranch El Aliso (in the vicinity of the present Los
Angeles Union Station) led the townsmen to call him Don Luis del Aliso. He
participated in the Battle of Cahuenga on February 20-21, 1845, which resulted in the deportation of Governor Micheltorena.

[94] Juan Castañeda, a native of Texas, came to California in 1837 as a captain, having previously held a command in Baja California.

[95] Narciso Durán, a Spanish friar who came to California in 1806 and
thereafter served for forty years as missionary, chiefly at San José and Santa
Barbara. Bancroft considered him one of the most prominent and influential
of the Franciscans.

point of Carpintería, situated about half way between Santa Barbara and San Buenaventura. I understood that this agreement was with the approval of Lieutenant Colonel Castro, who was in Santa Barbara awaiting the arrival of Governor Alvarado, who was expected there very shortly. But Señor Castro violated the agreement and one night arrived at San Buenaventura with a detachment and two pieces of artillery, suprising our people. Some of them managed to get out of the mission and went to Los Angeles, where they notified Governor Carrillo of what had happened. Carrillo issued a call to the neighboring towns through the alcaldes and all the people offered to accompany the governor on a march to San Buenaventura against the forces of Castro. Some twenty-five or thirty men gathered (I among them). I was named commandant of this force and under my orders were Ensign Don Ignacio del Valle[96] and Ensign Don Juan Salazar,[97] also Don José Sepúlveda, Don Juan Gallardo, and others. Before arriving at the Santa Clara river I encountered a man –

---

[96] Ignacio del Valle came to California with Echeandía; in 1828 he became a cadet officer in the Santa Barbara company, then going to San Diego to serve as ayudante de plaza. In 1831-32 he joined the insurrectionists against Victoria and Zamorano, although his father, a lieutenant, served on the other side. In 1833 he was commissioned to assist in the secularization of San Gabriel, Santa Cruz and San Francisco missions. He supported Gutiérrez against Alvarado in 1836, and after the downfall of Gutiérrez, he supported Governor Carrillo, which in turn resulted in his being sent to Sonoma as a prisoner, following the unsuccessful march on Santa Barbara. Later he returned to California and, on the death of his father, settled on the Rancho San Francisco on the Santa Clara river at the Rancho Camulos in Ventura County. He died in 1880.

[97] Juan Salazar commanded the guard at San Fernando mission in 1823, and from 1827-30 he was acting habilitado (paymaster and business agent) at Santa Barbara and San Diego. In 1846 he was acting commander of the San Diego Company.

one of those who had escaped San Buenaventura – and he told us that Señor Castro had made prisoners, the major part of our force that had been stationed there. With this news we returned to Los Angeles and upon arrival here, discovered that the governor had left for San Diego. I believe that upon his arrival there, a force was organized that went out in search of José Castro and his men. I seem to remember that Captain de la Portilla headed this force and that upon his arrival at San Luis Rey, he encountered Captain Don Juan José Tovar.[98] They stayed there a few days and the governor persuaded Tovar to take command of the forces. Señor Tovar was from Sonora and a captain of the Mexican army. When he met with the other officers in a council of war, he made it known that his coming to California had no other object but to make my acquaintance; with whom, much earlier, he had communicated in writing without our having known each other personally. He also made it known that because he was an officer of the Mexican army, he considered himself obligated to give his services to the lawful authorities who were soliciting it. After being recognized by all as *jefe,* including Portilla, because Tovar was older than he or because he was considered more capable, he undertook the command and began the campaign, going to Las Flores. There he encamped, leaving the governor at San Luis Rey. It was known that Castro's forces were approaching San Juan Capistrano.

On the same day that Tovar encamped, the governor

---

[98] Juan José Tovar came to California in 1838 from Sonora, apparently upon the request of Governor Carrillo. He had probably only a small escort, but Carrillo made the most of Tovar's arrival by announcing he had come to quell the disorders in California, and that he had brought a sufficient force.

set out for Las Flores about five or six p.m. Trujillo,[99] the secretary of government, remained at San Luis Rey, as well as Manuel Requeña, who had accompanied the governor from Los Angeles.

Before the governor left, Señor Trujillo had informed me confidentially that he (Carrillo) intended to recognize Alvarado as governor. I did not want to believe it and Señor Trujillo tried to persuade me to ask Carrillo. I did not ask such a question and contented myself solely with writing a note to Tovar and to my brother, Lieutenant José Antonio Pico, who had also joined the expedition, informing them that the governor was setting out with the intention of submitting to Señor Alvarado, and that they should be very careful. Carrillo had given me orders to assist Trujillo and Requeña with saddle and pack horses, so that they might journey to the border of Baja California. Also, he asked me to accompany him to the north. I offered to go but I did not. I sent him a confidential letter telling him that I had not gone with him because I knew that he intended to submit to Señor Alvarado.

The day after Carrillo arrived in Las Flores, the forces of Alvarado and Castro appeared, cutting off communications with San Diego, since Los Angeles was already insured. So-called Captain Don José Antonio de la Guerra y Carrillo,[100] remained at San Buena-

---

99 Manuel Trujillo, secretary to Governor Carrillo, left California with Tovar after the fracas at Los Flores.

100 José Antonio de la Guerra y Carrillo, born 1805, was the son of José de la Guerra y Noriega. He began life as a cadet in the Santa Barbara Company. He was involved in political and military matters during the Mexican period. In the American period he served terms as sheriff of San Luis Obispo County. He often signed his name José Noriega, which of course was legal. He and his wife, Maria Concepcion Ortega, had six children. Bancroft states, "[His] record was in several respects not the best, though there is nothing very bad to be said of him."

ventura with a small force, and Alvarado's and Castro's artillery pieces. Also there, confined as prisoners, were some of the force captured a short while earlier.

Immediately after I received information of the arrival of Castro and Alvarado at Las Flores, I left San Luis Rey accompanied only by one majordomo. When I was about a league from San Luis Rey, Francisco María Alvarado [101] (an escaped prisoner from San Buenaventura) arrived and informed me that Captain de la Guerra y Carrillo was unwell and that his force was small. We then agreed that he should go to San Diego to gather all the men he could. I should go and await them at San Dieguito. [102] The next day, Francisco María Alvarado appeared there with sixteen men. I told them of my intentions, that is to march to San Buenaventura with the intent of taking from Guerra the cannons that were in his charge.

I sent a note to Covarrubias, [103] who was at Las Flores,

[101] Francisco María Alvarado, grantee of Santa María Peñasquito Rancho northeast of La Jolla and Soledad Rancho at Del Mar, served several public offices: alcalde and regidor at Los Angeles, and treasurer of San Diego.

[102] San Dieguito Rancho, San Diego County. Two leagues were granted to to the Silva family in 1831, provisionally. In 1840 or '41 and 1845 it was granted to Juan María Osuna.

[103] José María Covarrubias, French born, a citizen of Mexico, came to California with the Híjar and Padrés colony as a teacher. He was *comisionado* for the secularization of Santa Ines in '36-37; was a partisan of Carrillo in the contest of '38, in which year he married into the Carrillo family; took part in the arrest of Americans of the Graham affair and escorted prisoners to San Blas. Covarrubias was grantee of Castac Rancho, secretary of the Assembly and alcalde of Santa Barbara in '44, and secretary to Pío Pico in '45. His visit to Santa Ines and conference with Fremont, when Fremont passed through on his march south, was not at the time looked upon favorably by defenders of California. In '49 he was a member of the Constitutional Convention, and of the first legislature under the United States, being four times re-elected; and he was county judge of Santa Barbara in '61. Honored and respected, he died in 1870 at the age of sixty-nine.

which I transmitted in a bag carried by an Indian fisherman. In this note I asked Tovar to refrain from having any transactions with the enemy; that I was marching to San Buenaventura as was previously planned and afterwards would come to his assistance from the rear. But my letter arrived late because Tovar's force had begun to desert, each one to his house. It had been discovered that Tovar's cannons were primed with charcoal dust instead of gun powder, which circumstance made everyone distrustful, and from that resulted the general dispersion.

When I was at the point of leaving San Dieguito, I saw at a distance some five or six men coming from San Luis Rey. I waited for them. They were Sergeant Julio Osuna [104] (my first cousin) and five or six soldiers who had escaped from Las Flores. I learned from them that Captain Tovar had also fled from there.

I decided to wait for Tovar and in a short while he arrived accompanied by two or three Sonorans. Together we returned to San Diego and from there we went to my ranch, Jamul, from whence Tovar left for Sonora.

After making an arrangement with Alvarado, Carrillo went with him to Santa Barbara.

I had no more news about Carrillo until some months afterwards he appeared one night at San Luis Rey in the company of his son, Don Pedro C. Carrillo,[105] and

[104] Julio Osuna, descendant of Teodoro Osuna and his Indian wife Laguarda Quisques, came to San Diego in the 1780s. Julio assumed control of San Dieguito Rancho after the death of his father Leandro Osuna. His wife was Josefa, daughter of Philip Crosthwaite, sheriff of San Diego County.

[105] Pedro C. Carrillo, son of Carlos Antonio, educated at Honolulu and Boston, was grantee of Alamos y Agua Caliente Rancho, and Camulos Rancho in 1843, and of San Diego Island Rancho in 1846. During the Mexican War

José María Covarrubias. They informed me that they had fled from Santa Barbara fearing mistreatment at the hands of Alvarado and Castro. I aided them with horses and all necessaries and they continued their flight to the border of Baja California.

I forgot to say that when our force was at San Buenaventura it had been engaged by that of Castro with guns and cannon. No one from our side was killed in this action. On Castro's side, one artilleryman, who was operating a piece of artillery in the south section, was killed. His name was Juan Cordero,[106] but he was better known by the nickname of Juan Cornado.

Having left San Luis Rey to spend the Christmas season with my family in San Diego, I again encountered Señor Carrillo, his son Pedro, and Señor Covarrubias. Also there were Don José Antonio Carrillo with my sister Estéfana, his wife. They both were staying at my home. Estéfana was sick and died – this was in 1838.

I went to San Diego to play the part of the devil in a *pastorela*.[107] This I did on the 25th of December and I believe it was at dawn of the 27th that Don José Castro arrived at San Diego with a force. The first one to be aroused at my house was Covarrubias, who saw Señor Castro. Covarrubias came to tell us that Señor Castro wishes to see us and that we should go to the house of Señor Bandini, where he was staying. We all went there. Castro then made it known that we were his pris-

---

he favored the Americans and was compensated by being appointed collector of the ports of San Pedro, San Diego and later Santa Barbara. At one time he was town surveyor of Santa Barbara, and later justice of the peace of Los Angeles.

[106] Of Juan Cordero, Bancroft merely mentions he was at Santa Barbara in 1837, married to Antonia Valenzuela, and had seven children.

[107] Pastorela: an Idyl, or poem in which the speakers act as shepherds.

oners. That same afternoon, he made us go with him
and his men to San Luis Rey.

After traveling six or seven leagues, we spent the
night at the San Dieguito ranch. The next day Castro
ordered me ahead to San Luis Rey to prepare provisions for his troops.

While at San Luis Rey, we prisoners contrived a
plan to free ourselves. The plan was to invite the alcalde of San Diego, José Antonio Estudillo, to come
with a force to help us obtain our freedom, making the
appointment for nine o'clock at night of the particular
day and [advising] the route by which they would be
able to enter the house where I was residing, which was
also the house where Castro and his three or four officers dwelt and ate. I remember one of them was
Joaquín de la Torre.[108]

We prisoners armed ourselves with daggers the night
we were to effect our project. Besides, I called five
majordomos from the mission and got ready five guns
in anticipation of arrival of the alcalde's expedition
from San Diego. Alcalde Estudillo fooled us. He stopped about a mile and a half from San Luis Rey and
there he remained until the next day when he and his
men returned to San Diego.

108 Joaquín de la Torre, educated in Monterey, was corporal in the Monterey Company in 1836. In 1840 he took an active part in the arrest of the
Americans (Graham affair) and accompanied the prisoners to San Blas.
Grantee of Arroyo Seco Rancho (located in Monterey County, west of Green-
field) in 1845, he was active in the campaign against Micheltorena; in 1846
he was in command of the troops sent by Castro to give battle to the Bear
Flag army, and got the worst of a skirmish at Olompali, but by deceiving Fremont by a ruse, he succeeded in crossing the bay and accompanied Castro
south. After the American occupation he was paroled, but broke his parole to
fight in the Natividad campaign. He was of much energy and courage, and
never friendly to the Americans. In 1855 he was killed by Anastasio García.

We, ourselves, waited until past nine o'clock when we began to doubt whether the alcalde was going to come and so resolved to carry out our plan, but Don José Antonio Carrillo suggested that we return to San Diego after seizing the officers; while I was of the opinion that we should continue the march in search of Governor Alvarado, so as to seize him as well. Because of this disagreement, the debate grew warm and, hearing that we were talking in somewhat of a commotion, Don Carlos Antonio Carrillo recommended to us very particularly not to do anything violent. The truth is, we had confided the project to him for fear he would oppose it, being a somewhat timid man despite his large stature.

Since our plan had been frustrated, we all remained on friendly terms, since Castro would have us believe that we were at liberty and that he was only taking us to have an interview with Governor Alvarado.

Carlos Antonio Carrillo was a man of great height and bulk – of handsome appearance and truly fine looking man; bushy beard and with very curly, black hair; fair, rosy complexion and large black eyes. He was in the habit of always keeping his head covered with a black handkerchief, tied with a knot in front and his hat way back of his head. He was a man of strong and capricious temperament. Some days he conducted himself as if he were a lunatic. When he was a soldier, or better said, when he was a corporal and a sergeant, he was exceedingly despotic – with those under his command. He never distinguished himself for valor, but he had the good luck of taking prisoner some of Bouchard's insurgents at Rancho del Refugio.

We remained at San Luis about four days and then

proceeded in the direction of Santa Barbara, by way of Los Angeles. We gave the appearance of being at liberty. At the rancho of Santa Ana, my brother Andrés (who was one of the prisoners, though I do not remember how or where he was captured) began to get suspicious and told me that he believed that this apparent liberty was just some of Castro's cunning – that in reality we were prisoners. He proposed to me that we escape and return to San Diego. I told him that we should not be distrustful, because in the main, nothing could happen to us even if we were being conducted as prisoners; that the only thing I feared was, that they might use force against an artilleryman named Guerra, and Antonio Avila [109] (who had also been taken prisoner at San Diego). Consequently, we should tell them that it would be wise for them to escape. Castro was afraid of these two men because they were brave and determined.

Avila was in California as a condition of banishment and came to this place with the famous Vicente Gómez, *El Capador*.[110]

Andrés advised Avila and Guerra that they should escape and gave a blanket to the latter. I do not remember what became of Avila, but Guerra was unable to escape and arrived with us at Santa Barbara. There were about three ships in the port when we arrived. We were made to halt on the wharf, surrounded by their

---

[109] Antonio Avila was banished to California in 1825, as a sentence of punishment for robberies and murder in Puebla, Mexico. In the Solís revolt of 1829, and during Zamorano's regime in 1832, he aided the government in hope of gaining a release, but had to remain and serve out his time until 1838.

[110] Vicente Gómez, a Mexican guerrillero-chief in the war of Independence, with the reputation of being a fiend, hence *El Capador*. He remained in California briefly, a few months at most.

force, and told that we must board these ships. We were scattered amongst the ships. I later learned that Guerra had been expelled from the country.

We were aboard a few days and then placed at liberty without further investigation. After eight days my brother and I returned to our homes. Carlos Antonio Carrillo and his son remained in Santa Barbara.

After this, Governor Alvarado, whose authority all this time had not been recognized by the people of San Diego, sent Don José Antonio Carrillo to tell me that all was now concluded; that the revolution had been terminated, because his commission as provisional governor had come, and now he desired to embrace me as a friend. I left San Diego with Carrillo for San Fernando, where Alvarado and his force were staying. I was received very cordially by Alvarado and we embraced. We had long conversations about past events, particularly those that occurred after the revolution against Victoria, as Alvarado had been my government secretary during my political leadership.

On leaving that afternoon, we embraced again and I offered him my services as a friend as well as the administrator of San Luis Rey.

I returned to Los Angeles to the home of my brother-in-law, José Antonio Carrillo. Two days later I was taken seriously ill. I was bedridden when Captain José María Villavicencio arrived with forty men. When Carrillo learned that the captain was drawing near, he told me that he probably was coming to take us prisoners. I counseled him to flee – that for my part, I had no recourse because of my inability to ride a horse. He did not want to abandon me and he stayed. A servant of mine also promised to defend me, so that I would not

be taken while ill. They immediately started to prepare
their arms.

I called Carrillo and begged him to leave, promising
him that I would hide. With this guarantee, he left, but
not telling me for where.

I summoned an intimate friend of mine, Teodosio
Yorba,[111] and asked him for his clothes to disguise myself. After putting them on, I went out on the street and
made my way to the home of my sister, Isidora, where
there was a place to hide.

Captain Villavicencio[112] came at last and took possession of José Antonio Carrillo's house, which was
situated where the hotel "Pico House" now stands. On
the other side of the same street there lived a Señor
Baric.[113] Carrillo hid himself there, behind a stairway.
Unfortunately, he was seen by one of the Baric's children who innocently informed the captain's people.
They went to get him out. I was hiding in a small attic
of my sister's house. Three or four times parties of
fifteen men sent by Captain Manuel Cota[114] came to
search the house without finding me. Don José Sepúl-

111 Teodosio Yorba at the time of this incident was only twenty-two years
old. He had an honorable life in varied official activities.

112 José María Villavicencio, generally known as Villa, a half Indian, was
adopted by Don Carlos A. Carrillo and his wife. During the Alvarado revolt
of 1836-38, he was at times in command at Santa Barbara. After being acting
prefect at Monterey, 1840, he was grantee of a rancho near San Luis Obispo.
Villavicencio saw service against the United States in 1846 at San Diego.
Later he was a prosperous rancher near San Luis Obispo.

113 Charles Baric, a Frenchman who came to California in 1834 with the
Híjar and Padrés colony, became a trader in Los Angeles. During the Alvarado revolt he aided Bandini in the capture of Los Angeles.

114 Manuel Cota – there were a father and son of the same name: Bancroft
lists a Lieutenant Manuel Cota under Victoria in 1839, however, the name
Manuel may have been a slip-of-the-tongue by Pico, and possibly he meant to
say Valentín Cota, who befriended him later. Manuel and Valentín were
possibly brothers.

veda had assured them that I must be there as I had been seen going in but not coming out.

In the deplorable state of health in which I found myself, it was not possible for me to endure longer the narrowness of my hiding place and the next time Cota came I gave myself up. He conducted me to Carrillo's house where the military force was lodged. There I met Carrillo, Ensign José María Ramirez,[115] Alcalde Gil Ibarra, and the secretary of the ayuntamiento, Narciso Botello.[116]

Immediately after that I went to bed. Señor Sepúlveda, Antonio Ignacio Avila,[117] and his son, Juan,[118] came to see me. These three told Villavicencio that I was gravely ill and asked permission to take me to one

---

[115] José María Ramirez, came to California in 1825 with Governor Echeandía and was attached to the San Diego Company until about 1830. He married Dolores Palomares in 1830 and was tried and acquitted of bigamy. He took part in the revolt of 1831, was named *comisionado* to secularize San Diego Mission in 1833-34, and served later in connection with Santa Ines. He was involved in the sectional quarrels of 1837-38, being several times arrested in Southern California.

[116] Narciso Botello, a native of Alamos, Sonora, came to California with John Forster in 1833. He soon opened a grocery in Los Angeles, where he became síndico of the ayuntamiento in 1835, its secretary in 1836, and an active opponent of Alvarado in 1836-38, giving assistance to Bandini and the group associated with him. During the Mexican War he aided Flores against the Americans. In the American years he was a justice of the peace. He was a man of good abilities and fair education, always a partisan for his country, Mexico, against the U.S. In 1863 he dictated for Bancroft his "Anales del Sur," a very valuable narrative of his experience in the political and other complications in California.

[117] Antonio Ignacio Avila, a native of Sonora, came to California in 1783 and settled in Los Angeles. In 1804 married Rosa Ruíz. Grantee of Sauzal Redondo Rancho, he was prominent in the pursuit of Indian horse thieves. He died in 1858 at age seventy-four.

[118] Juan Avila was a grantee of Miguel Rancho. In 1847 he carried a flag of truce for Stockton to the people of Los Angeles. He married Soledad Yorba. He was a man of excellent repute, who avoided political complications. In 1877 he dictated his "Notas Californianas" for Bancroft.

of their homes. Villavicencio refused, alleging that he had orders from the governor to take me, dead or alive. On learning this, I sent for Villavicencio and told him that if he did not trust me, to put me in jail with fetters for better security. He answered me as he had the others – that he could not wait and I had to go. Nevertheless, he offered to wait one more day. I refused his offer and got ready to leave. A few hours later, about two o'clock p.m., we started for Santa Barbara. On arriving there, we were imprisoned. We were confined in the same cell where Don Ignacio del Valle was kept in fetters. Later, to prevent our going any place, a chamber pot was ordered for each of the prisoners. My sister, Concepción, brought me a bed and I lay in it, half dead.

Three days later I called for Captain Valentín Cota,[119] with whom I had friendly relations and whom I thought a man of influence in his party. Cota came and I begged him to ask the governor to permit me to attend to my personal needs outside of that room. The captain returned about eight o'clock that night and told me my request had been granted. I put on my cape and went out. At the door were two armed soldiers, who had me march between them some ten or twelve paces, then stopped so that I could attend to my natural needs. Of course, I could do nothing and my supplications for them to move away were to no avail. I returned again to my bed.

Around ten o'clock that same night, Don Valentín Cota returned and informed me that he had just come

---

119 Valentín Cota, son of Manuel (who may or may not be the Manuel in footnote 114), was captain of Santa Barbara Company, and supported Alvarado in the 1836-38 affair. He was grantee of Río Santa Clara Rancho in 1837. His wife was Luz González.

from a war council of Castro and his officers, in which they had decided to leave the next morning for Sonora with the prisoners.

I had forgotten to mention that when we arrived in Santa Barbara, I saw Don Mariano G. Vallejo, José Castro, Juan B. Alvarado, and some others on the balcony of the house where they were lodged. That was the first and last time I saw Señor Vallejo in the south since the uprising against Gutiérrez. I was carrying a dagger in my boot, with Captain Villavicencio's permission, and from the balcony above, José Castro ordered an officer to take the dagger from me. They took it and I never saw it again.

Cota gave me the welcome news that he had managed to have them allow me to stay in Santa Barbara because of my illness and in my place take my brother, Andrés, who was staying there at the time. But this last about my brother, he had not told me. Anyway, I did not believe anything and I ordered my servant to have my horse ready early in the morning. They got Andrés out of bed in the morning and took him to where the prisoners were. In a short while a member of the military came to inform me that I did not have to go north. After that, he gave orders to my brother to get ready to leave for the north with the prisoners. Then I gave him my saddled horse and the prisoners left that same day. Afterward, they permitted me to move to my sister's house, having the presidio as a prison.

A few days later, after I had recovered, I was invited to be a godfather to a baby. The mother of this baby, I believe, was a relative of Alvarado and asked for and received permission for me to go to the Santa Barbara Mission for the christening.

Alvarado, himself, came in the carriage of Father President Narciso Durán to take me to the mission. Upon arrival, we were met by a force lined on one side of the church, and while we were getting out of the carriage the troops fired a volley in salute. Alvarado conducted me to a room in the house of the padres, where the officers were. There he presented me with about two hundred dollars in silver for my services as godfather. I accepted it and we then went together to the church where the baptismal ceremony was performed. This concluded, the governor returned me to my sister's home.

While I was still detained at the presidio, I received the news that heathen Indians had attacked my ranch, Jamul, killing the majordomo and four *vaqueros,* taking two of the majordomo's unmarried daughters with them. His wife they had let go, disrobed – burning the house and taking with them everything that was of value of mine and of my family. Moreover, all my horses and nearly two thousand head of cattle. Fortunately, my family was in San Diego. I made this known to Señor Alvarado and he immediately set me at liberty to go and tend to my affairs.

Some time later, a force of soldiers under the command of Ensign Macedonio González [120] left in pursuit of those Indians. It was said that González was brave and very experienced in campaigns against Indians. But the truth is, that the Indians defeated the troops at Jacum,[121] nearly killing González, and took fourteen

---

120 Macedonio González was a Mexican half-breed on the Baja California frontier, with a reputation of being a famous Indian fighter. He took part with the *sureños* (southerners) in the troubles of 1837-40.

saddled horses from the soldiers. The terrain was not suited for attacking on horseback, so the soldiers left the horses at a distance, guarded by two men. The Indians overcame these two and succeeded in taking fourteen horses. González, a corporal of the San Diego Company named Cristóbal Duarte,[122] and a soldier, Joaquín Soto,[123] were seriously wounded.

In 1840, I was *vocal* of the *Diputación* or Assembly and was in Monterey. My colleagues were Captain Santiago Argüello, Don Rafael González [124]– I don't remember who the other two were with whom we formed a quorum. I and the two above-named agreed to make a proposal so that the assemblymen would go to Los Angeles to hold their sessions because it was the capital of the Department of California. Governor Alvarado, who was presiding, objected and then the deputies Argüello and González refused to back my proposal and sided with the governor. This was during the first session.

The second session was presided over by Don Manuel Jimeno,[125] first vocal. The discussion of my proposal

[121] Jacum (also spelled Jacom) refers to the Jacumba Mountains, Valley and Hot Springs some sixty-five miles east of San Diego on the California-Mexican border. The name is derived from *La Rancheria Llamada en su idioma Jacom* (the village called Jacom in their [Diegueño] language).

[122] Of Cristóbal Duarte no mention is made in Bancroft's *Register*.

[123] Joaquín Soto, soldier in San Diego County, came to California in 1836.

[124] Rafael González, came to California with Figueroa in 1833 as Mexican administrator of customs. Aside from serving at the customs house for a number of years, he was also a member of the junta 1839-43, and a grantee of Rancho San Buenaventura Misión and San Miguelito. Larkin reported him a man of property and influence. Bancroft summarizes him as of good character, but ignorant. In 1878 he gave his narrative, "Experiencias," to Bancroft. He died in Monterey in 1868 at the age of eighty-two.

[125] Manuel Jimeno, listed in Bancroft as Manuel Jimeno Casarino, came to

continued, with the result that I was forced to tell them
emphatically that in flattering the governor, they were
failing their duty. These deputies complained to the
governor that I had offended them.

The third session was again presided over by Governor Alvarado. The discussions that continued were
concerned with González and Argüello's complaint
that I had not only insulted them, but I had violated
parliamentary rules. I promptly replied by repeating
what I had said and maintaining that they were down-
right flatterers of the governor and that if the law was
not complied with, I would not attend any more of the
sessions but would withdraw and inform the central
government. The result was the chairman ordered me
confined to my room and imposed on me a fine of two
hundred dollars, although later he relieved me of pay-
ing it.

I was confined several days until it was discovered
what the foreigners were plotting. The governor sent
me a summons declaring that the country was threatened by a foreign invasion. Thinking that my services
as deputy would certainly be of use, I offered them
gladly, stipulating that when this matter of the pacification of the country was concluded, I would again
withdraw from the sessions. That is what I did as soon

California in 1828 from Mexico, and was a brother of Father José J. Jimeno
(who incidentally is the prototype of Father Salvaderra of Helen Hunt Jack-
son's *Ramona*). He served under Alvarado as secretary of state, senior member of the assembly, and on several occasions acted governor pro-tem. In 1832
he married Doña Angustias de la Guerra (who later married Dr. James L.
Ord, and in 1878 related to Thomas Savage, her *Occurrences in California*).
He was a grantee of three ranchos, namely Santa Paula (Ventura County),
Jimeno Rancho (Colusa County), and Salsipuedes Rancho (Santa Cruz County). However, he did not appear as a claimant for any of these before he
went to Mexico in 1853, where he died the same year.

as this business was concluded, with the expulsion to Mexico, as prisoners, those who were accused of being the ring leaders in the plan against the government. I always have been of the belief that this conspiracy never existed, and I base this on the fact that I, myself (according to what Father José María Suárez del Real [126] told me), was accused of complicity in it when this was false to the point of my not even knowing the foreigners who were accused of having formulated such a plot.

At the conclusion of this matter, I retired to my home in San Luis Rey, being that the mission was under my care. That same year of 1840, Señor Alvarado relieved me of its administration and I delivered it on his orders to Don José Antonio Estudillo.

THE MISSION OF SAN LUIS REY

When I took charge of the administration of San Luis Rey, receiving it from the hands of Captain Don Pablo de la Portilla, I imposed the condition on Jefe Político Figueroa that I be allowed to govern the Indians the same as they had been governed before by the padres, as the Indians were disorganized and only in this manner could I bring order. Also, it was agreed that the government would not require of the establishment any kind of contributions during the entire time of my administration because I considered that all this property belonged by right and justice to the Indians.

---

[126] Father José María Suárez del Real, brother of Father Antonio Suárez del Real, came to California in 1833, and served first as missionary at Mission San Carlos (Carmel), then priest at Santa Clara, and later was in charge at San José and San Carlos in 1844. Bancroft's evaluation of him is most adverse, whereas he states, "Padre José María somewhat resembled his brother in character, though an abler man, with more skill in concealing his irregularities. (Their conduct) was most unfortunate for the general reputation of the California padres – a most excellent body of men."

Señor Figueroa acceded to all. The 21st or 25th of
April, 1835, I commenced my administration. I received some fifteen thousand sheep. There was not one
horse, nor one mule, nor any tame animals. All the cattle were wild and scattered. Complete disorder reigned
in the mission.

I dedicated myself with great zeal to the job, and in
a short time I succeeded in bringing order out of chaos.
I had all the buildings repaired, which were even without doors. The first thing I did was to send eight of my
own mules, perfectly equipped, to the Mission of San
Fernando to buy, with my own money, corn for planting. I sent a request to my mother at San Diego for four
fanegas [127] of beans for the same purpose. With this I
started the planting.

I had the good fortune to have still alive at that time,
some of the majordomos that served in the establishment at the time of Father Antonio Peyri: [128] Antonio
Chorbi, Mexican; Tomás Serrano, [129] Tomás Gutiérrez, [130] Antonio Valenzuela, [131] and Joaquín Velásquez.
At the time they accepted their charge as majordomos,
I instructed them that they should perform their duties
as they had at the time of Father Peyri. This authorized

---

127 A fanega is approximately two bushels.

128 Antonio Peyri, Spanish friar who came to California in 1796, served at
Mission San Luis Obispo and founder of San Luis Rey. He returned to Spain
in 1836.

129 Tomás Serrano appears as *Juez de Campo* (judge of the plains) at
Los Angeles in 1848. His duties were to preside over each rodeo, settle disagreements involving ownership of cattle, interpret rules and customs, order
the arrest of cattle thieves and "vagrants, vagabonds and dangerous and suspicious persons." This office was one of recognized dignity and responsibility.

130 Tomás Gutiérrez was a grantee of land at San Juan Capistrano in 1841.

131 Antonio Valenzuela was grantee of land at San Juan Capistrano in
1841, at San Gabriel in 1843, and again at San Gabriel in 1846.

them to punish the Indians when they neglected their duties.

The first arbitrary act I committed, the day after taking charge of the establishment, was to order a pair of fetters put on the first alcalde and to give him fifty lashes, while tied to a post. His offense was that he violently attacked the majordomo who had given him certain orders pertaining to the work. Señor Figueroa was in the establishment at the time and did not intervene. From that day on I did not have occasion to punish any of the Indians for a long time, and even then, the punishments were given on orders from the government.

During the second temporary administration of Gutiérrez, the Indians of San Luis Rey wanted to start an uprising against me, protesting that I had disposed of the skins and tallow of the mission. When I learned this, I took precautions and was informed that the ringleader of the scheme was an Indian named Pablito who knew how to read and write. I had him come to my office and I asked him if he was the promoter of the plot that was to be carried out the next day, Sunday, while we would be at mass. He confessed to me that he was, and that the alcaldes themselves had brought him from Rancho Temecula to inform him of what they had planned, which was to make him administrator after seizing me and the soldiers of the guard. Around five o'clock p.m., one of the Indians came and told me that they were gathering in their quarters for the purpose of coming to see what steps I was taking in respect to Pablito. At this news, I ordered that Sergeant Pablo Rodríguez, commander of the guard, be called and there, face to face, he confirmed to me what Pablito had said. He learned of it from one of the Indian alcaldes with whom he was on friendly terms and who was no other than the father of Pablito. At sundown, a major-domo came and advised me that a multitude of Indians armed with arrows was approaching. I sent for another majordomo and one of my servants. I armed them with guns and stationed them in my office. The moment the door was opened to send the sergeant back to the guard-house, there was in front, between the guardhouse and my residence, a large multitude of Indians in a hostile attitude, which obliged the sergeant to get back into the office. I took precautionary and defensive measures for the safety of my family and the others who were in the house.

About eleven o'clock p.m. I decided to appear at the door of the house in front of which were the hostile Indians, and I ordered them to return to their homes. Some of them who spoke Spanish replied that they would not go back without taking Pablito with them; that he should be the administrator and not I; that if I did not set him at liberty, they would take him by force. I refused their demands telling them to do what they wished.

After a short while, I spoke to them a second time, with the same effect. They refused to obey, daring me to fire my pistols, threatening to seize me as soon as I fired.

About one or two o'clock in the morning I ordered Sergeant Rodríguez to tell them for the third time to withdraw to their homes. They continued to refuse to obey, insisting on taking Pablito with them.

The sergeant counseled me to let him go to prevent

more serious consequences. I went out with Pablito and turned him over to the crowd, which might have been about eight hundred or one thousand Indians. They left immediately, taking him to their quarters.

Next day, around eight or nine o'clock a.m., about sixty Indians appeared, preceded by their alcaldes, and told me that they came in the name of all the Indians to beg me to forgive them and to inform me that they recognized me as the administrator. To this I replied that by no means would I consent to be their administrator until they were convinced of the legality of all my acts. I asked them which of their majordomos they wished to have administer their interests. They replied it should be Tomás Gutiérrez. An alcalde looked for him and brought him to my presence. He refused to accept the responsibility. Then I suggested that they reach an understanding with their alcaldes, until I was vindicated. They then asked permission to get in touch with the chief, who was at San Gabriel, and with Don Pablo de la Portilla, whom they still believed authorized to take charge of the mission. I granted all their requests. They sent letters to both. I, too, made the circumstances known to the superior authorities. They ordered me to take charge of managing the establishment and, if necessary, maintain authority with force; that if the force there was not sufficient, to ask for aid from the guard at San Juan Capistrano and to proceed to arrest the ring leaders of the movement and punish them as I saw fit, promising me to be at the mission by a certain day within the next seven or eight days. I summoned the guard from San Juan and they stayed several days at San Luis.

Upon receiving Señor Gutiérrez's orders, I called all

the alcaldes and made known to them the disposition of the authorities, ordering them to send a message to each one of the ranches, namely: Pala,[132] Temecula,[133] San Jacinto,[134] San Jose,[135] advising the Indians to come to the mission on a certain day. They came on the designated day, and Sunday morning I asked the sergeant if he could proceed to carry out the government's order with the men he had. He answered affirmatively and we immediately proceeded to comply with it.

It was the custom to have the Indians gather in the plaza of the seminary at the conclusion of the mass. That is what they did. Immediately after the alcaldes notified me of this, I ordered the alcaldes to go to the guardhouse to inform the sergeant. He and I had decided to put fetters on each one and lock them in a cell, and so it was done.

Sergeant Rodríguez kept ready his twenty-five armed men, twenty of whom were posted in the warehouse,

132 The Valley of Pala situated forty-five miles north of San Diego. Here was located Asistencia de San Antonio de Pala, founded in 1816 by Father Peyri. The evicted Palatinguas from Warner's Ranch now occupy an Indian reservation there.

133 Temecula, a rancho in present Riverside County, was granted in 1835 to José Antonio Estudillo, to be rejected later. Provisionally granted in 1840 to Andrés and Pío Pico, who asked for its exchange for Santa Margarita, however, no exchange was made. In 1844 the rancho was granted to Félix Valdez by Governor Manuel Micheltorena, a total of 26,608.94 acres.

134 San Jacinto. What Pico apparently refers to is all (or part) of the four ranchos located in present Riverside County, under the jurisdiction of San Luis Rey Mission. They are San Jacinto Nuevo y Potrero (at Lakeview), San Jacinto y San Gregorio (near Beaumont), San Jacinto Viejo (at San Jacinto and Hemet), and Sobrante de [residue of] San Jacinto Viejo y Nuevo (at Perris).

135 San José, properly named San José del Valle (or) Agua Caliente, in San Diego County at Warner Springs. In 1840, eleven leagues were granted to José Antonio Bernardino Pico, then regranted in 1844 to Jonathan Trumbull Warner.

retaining only five with a small piece of artillery in the guardhouse. I then ordered the twenty armed men to take their positions in the doorway that led to the plaza of the seminary. I came out and in a loud voice read the government's order to punish the ring leaders. I called Agustín, an Indian who had served as a courier in the riot, and ordered him whipped. But the rest did not want to permit the punishment. After reasoning with them, they agreed that I should punish him. Then I told them that I did not want to punish him, now that they had agreed to it. I allowed Agustín to go free. I ordered the door to the plaza opened, and all the Indians put out, and the twenty soldiers to return to their quarters.

On learning that their alcaldes were prisoners, the Indians wanted to attack the guard but Rodríguez told them not to pass a certain point or he would fire. Nothing happened even though the Indians remained, grumbling, nearly an hour. At last I went out and told them through an interpreter that they should leave and present their complaints, if they had any, the next day when the general should arrive and then everything would be taken care of.

Señor Gutiérrez did arrive the next day and we agreed to call the Indians together the following Sunday. On Saturday they all came from the ranches. Also present at the time were Captain Portilla and the alcalde of San Diego, Don Santiago Argüello, who had come to my aid.

After mass Sunday, the Indians gathered in the plaza. The comandante-general appeared in full uniform accompanied by Don Pablo and Don Santiago.

When they were at the plaza, as well as myself, I called the Indian interpreter and told him to let all the Indians know that the general was there to hear their complaints against me. Two of the Indians came forward and the general, at my request, asked them what complaints they had. One of them alleged that he had no complaint against me other than that I had ordered the matron of the Nuns to punish one of his daughters. I explained the reason for the punishment was that she had run away from the nunnery with a young man.

The second Indian accused me of having sold the skins and tallow of the establishment. I called the interpreter and ordered him to tell all the people that right there was the one who had ordered me to send all the skins and tallow to San Diego, and to ask him for an accounting. The Indians became terribly violent and several times called Señor Gutiérrez a thief, cross-eyed, and several other insulting names. He threatened them by saying he had fifty men there to keep order, but he did not succeed, and preferring to leave, he withdrew without imposing any punishment whatever.

I stayed at the plaza with the majordomos and alcaldes to plan the work for the coming week. Nothing new occurred. Next day, the Indians went peacefully back to their duties. Matters continued so until I turned over the administration in 1840. I was convinced that all of this was incited by certain individuals who envied my position. The truth is, that since Alvarado's revolution when all the missions were completely demoralized, only in San Luis Rey was order maintained. Not a single individual, white or Indian, came to it without his passport because, although for some time I did not recognize Alvarado as governor, I complied with all his commands pertaining to the preservation of order.

At least I had the satisfaction of turning over the buildings in perfect condition, whitewashed inside and out; a shoemaker's shop which I myself established; two blacksmiths' and one carpenter's shop with all their tools; a soap manufactory completely furnished; a loom with forty carders, ten weavers, ninety to one hundred girls occupied at the spinning wheels, working with pleasure as they sang all day; twenty-five thousand sheep; one hundred and twenty-five mules – of these, forty fully equipped with saddles; around two hundred tame horses, about fifty tame mares and some two hundred wild mares; more than three thousand head of cattle; about forty yokes of oxen and some domesticated cows with unweaned calves. The troops of Pala, Temecula, San Jacinto, and San José were left well supplied with wheat, barley, corn, peas, and beans. At Pala there was also much lima beans.

All of the debts incurred during my administration were liquidated. I left no debts pending and I canceled much that was owed by a few poor farm workers.

During my administration I succeeded in securing approval from the government of Señor Alvarado that each of the Indians who founded the pueblo of Las Flores [136] be given a yoke of oxen or a mule, besides two hundred and fifty head of cattle for the community. But

---

[136] Las Flores. In 1822 the Mission San Luis Rey established an asistencia near the ocean. About three hundred Indians lived in adobe and brush huts, making a good-sized village called "the flowers." After secularization of the mission in 1834, Las Flores became a *pueblo libre,* or free town, under Indian control, and it remained as such until after the Picos took over Rancho Santa Margarita. The site is north of Oceanside on the U.S. Marine Corps property – Camp Joseph H. Pendleton.

it is a deplorable fact that when General Micheltorena [137] came in 1842, these Indians no longer had any
of these goods, nor anything to eat, and the majority of
them had gone to the mountains. I took advantage of
this circumstance to buy from the remainder their
equity in the town, with the approval of the superior
authorities.

One year after I turned over San Luis Rey, there remained nothing but a small amount of the liquor that
was being manufactured. Plenty of cattle remained but
the rest had disappeared, with the exception of wild
livestock, and the worst disorder reigned in the establishment.

I had forgotten to relate a curious occurrence that
took place when Commandante-General Gutiérrez and
various officers who accompanied him came to the mission. As I knew the weaknesses of these gentlemen,
before they arrived I summoned the alcaldes and
ordered them not to permit any of the Indian boys or
girls to walk in the corridors of the mission after sunset – all should remain in their respective quarters

137 Manuel Micheltorena was brigadier-general in the Mexican army and
governor of California 1842-45. Historian Eldredge characterizes him as
". . . in the main, a well meaning ruler, and his courtesy and friendly
attitude towards foreigners, to whom he made many grants of land, made him
very popular with them. He is best remembered in California by the army of
jail birds he brought into it and by his connection with the Limantour fraud."
Bancroft states, ". . . he was a strange mixture of good and bad; a most
fascinating and popular gentleman; honest, skilful, and efficient as an official
in minor matters; utterly weak, unreliable, and even dishonorable in all emer-
gencies; yet under ordinary circumstances, by reason of his intelligence, experience, and tact in winning friends, he might have been a good ruler for
California. By his liberality in granting lands, as well as by his personal
courtesy, he made a good impression on most foreigners, who as a rule have
given an unfair version of the revolution by which he was overthrown. After
leaving California he took a somewhat prominent part in the war against the
U.S. in 1847, and commanding-general of Yucatán in 1850."

while the general and his forces remained there, so that nothing should happen to them.

Gutiérrez and his officers would see the girls working in the shops and, come nightfall, would ask for them. They were told that they were all at home with their parents, which was not true as the single girls were locked up in the women's quarters, and I had the key at my house so that they could not bribe the one who took care of them. After four or five days, seeing they could not contact the young Indian girls in Santa Inés, they told me they wanted to go to Pala and I accompanied them. After wine was prepared for them, that afternoon I had the alcaldes bring the Indians to meet the general and his officers. They drank the wine and then the idea occurred to me to take from Gutiérrez and his officers all the money they carried. And that's what I did. I borrowed all their silver and threw it to the Indians in honor of the visit of these gentlemen. That night they asked me for money so that they could go amongst the Indians, but I assured them I did not have so much as a *real,* and that I would return their money at the mission. In conversation, I told them that I surmised the object of their visit to Pala and was determined that they should have no money with which to bring disorder amongst the Indian women and, perhaps, even worse things. They resigned themselves and returned to the mission, and from there to Monterey without achieving their objective.

GOVERNOR MICHELTORENA, 1842-1845

From the time of my separation from the ex-mission of San Luis Rey until the end of Alvarado's administration, I did not involve myself in public affairs. Nor did I want to take part in the assembly of which I was a voting member. After the arrival of General Michel-torena, which occurred in 1842, I occupied myself anew with my duties as first voting member of the assembly.

I was summoned by General Micheltorena in 1844. Lieutenant Colonel Castro was in Monterey and was commander of the company garrisoned there. At the special request of Señor Micheltorena, my brother, Don Andrés, came expressly to Los Angeles to take me to Monterey. I went with him and on arriving I visited the general, accompanied by my brother.

During this visit the general made several observations that made me suspect he, in coalition with Señor Sutter,[138] had intentions of effecting the independence of this country with the expectation of thus improving the happiness and prosperity of its inhabitants. This was nothing more than mere suspicion, but at that moment it took possession of my mind and caused me much disquietude because I had always supported the integrity of Mexican territory. Besides, I was convinced that the country did not possess the necessary elements for independence and if it separated itself from Mexico, it would not be long before it would fall into the hands of another nation.

---

138 John August Sutter, a Swiss, came to America in 1834, and to California in 1839. Governor Alvarado granted him the "Establecimiento de Nueva Hel-vecia," eleven leagues (48,800 acres) on the Sacramento River where Sutter built his fort which occupied a rather strategic position, for it proved to be a mecca for those hundreds of immigrants pouring in from the East. Here the families, exhausted and half starved, as many of them were, found shelter, food and clothing, and importantly, work was available for all in Sutter's various interests. What cut short the role of Sutter being a benevolent host, was the discovery of gold at Coloma in 1848. What Pico has reference to, is Sutter's active participation in a campaign in 1844-45, when he assisted Micheltorena against the rebel forces under Pico and Alvarado.

Around August or September 1844, my brother, Don
Andrés, came to Los Angeles, commissioned by the
comandante-general to reorganize the presidial company garrisoned at San Diego, which had been discon-
tinued for several years. He brought an official communication directing me to organize the first civilian
squadron of Los Angeles, of which the general had appointed me its commandant upon his arrival in California. He instructed me to act in accordance with the
instructions he had given my brother, Andrés Pico, who
was commandant of the San Diego Company he was to
reorganize. Part of these instructions authorized us to
dispose of the property of the missions, to the point of
selling them, and to use the proceeds for the afore-
mentioned organizations.

Upon my arrival at Los Angeles, I got in touch with
the ayuntamiento in order to carry out the orders from
the government.

In consequence of the influence of Don Juan Bandini
and Señor Manuel Requeña, there was quite a bit of
opposition from the town to the organization of a
squadron, to the point of attempting to take possession
of the barracks in which my brother was stationed with
the fifty soldiers he had been able to recruit. In a hostile
attitude, the townspeople came to a distance of about
two hundred *varas* * from the barracks which was, at
the time, at the curate's house. Don Andrés assumed a
defensive attitude and brought out a piece of artillery
in front of the barracks. He marked a line past which
he admonished them not to come or he would fire. The
townspeople restrained themselves and afterwards I

* Vara: a Spanish measure of length, approximately 33 inches.

succeeded in pacifying the disgruntled ones, making them realize the necessity and advantages of the measures dictated by the government.

There were no more difficulties; on the contrary, I busied myself in looking for buyers of the San Juan Capistrano Mission with the hope of obtaining money. I left Los Angeles for that establishment accompanied by a commission named by Don Andrés Pico, which was composed of Don Antonio María Lugo and Don Francisco Sepúlveda.[139] Don Juan Temple,[140] who had the idea of buying the property if he liked it, also accompanied us.

The day after arriving at the ex-mission, I received an official letter from Don José Castro, who had arrived in Los Angeles with armed troops, notifying me of the critical circumstances of the country and the necessity of presenting myself immediately in Los Angeles. I returned at once and on my arrival learned that on the night before, Castro's troops had attacked the barracks

---

[139] Francisco Sepúlveda was the father of the prominent Sepúlveda clan featured in the annals of regional Los Angeles. Born in 1790 he came to California as a soldier in 1818. In 1825 he is mentioned as regidor and acting alcalde. During the 1831 fracas with Victoria he aided Pío Pico in the revolt, and as a consequence was imprisoned. In 1836 he was appointed comisionado of San Juan Capistrano. When 49 years of age he was a grantee of Rancho San Vicente y Santa Monica (Los Angeles County), but later having lost the papers, the rancho was re-granted to him by Governor Pío Pico.

[140] John (Don Juan) Temple was born in Massachusetts, in 1827 came to California, and shortly later married Rafaela, daughter of Francisco Cota. For some years thereafter he operated the first general merchandise store in Los Angeles (incidentally the first Vigilance Committee was organized in this store). Temple did not, however, take part in sectional quarrels. In time he became a creditor of several southern missions, and an owner of Rancho Los Cerritos (Los Angeles County). Harris Newmark pictures him as "known as one of the wealthiest, yet one of the stingiest men in all California. His real estate holdings around Los Angeles were enormous." He died May 31, 1866.

in which were the six or seven men of my brother's company. Castro had about one hundred men.

This dispute resulted, on Castro's side, in the death of a soldier named Juan Tamber [141] and the wounding of Ensign Joaquín de la Torre – and on Don Andrés' side, one soldier died, José María Barreras, who jumped the fence to flee. He was caught by Castro's soldiers and beheaded. This happened after the battle, therefore deserves to be considered a murder in cold blood.

In the first interview I had with Castro, he informed me that the cause of his coming to the south was that a riot against Micheltorena had taken place in the vicinity of Monterey. It had to do with the abuses and crimes continually committed by the troops of the permanent battalion that had come with the general from Mexico; that after the rebellion he and Micheltorena had a meeting and reached an agreement wherein the latter would have the soldiers of the battalion against whom complaints had been made leave the territory; that instead of complying with what had been promised he occupied himself, together with Captain Sutter, in organizing a force of eighty or more foreigners and another of about one hundred Indians; that considering the forces of Micheltorena superior to his, he was compelled to journey to the south; that under the circumstances that existed in the country, I, as first voting member of the assembly, should join them; and that they would recognize me as their legitimate governor. I did not agree to what had been proposed, but I offered

---

[141] Juan Tamber. This name is confusing. Bancroft lists Tambór (not Tamber) as a nickname. Thus he was "Juan the drummer" – the drummer-boy of Pico's forces.

to convoke the assembly with a view that they, as repre-
sentatives of the towns, should decide what was best for
the good of the country. I complied with my promise.
The chamber gathered in majority. Present were Don
Francisco de la Guerra,[142] Don Carlos A. Carrillo, Don
Francisco Figueroa,[143] Don Narciso Botello, and I. We
named Don Agustín Olvera[144] secretary.

The chamber decided to send a commission to General Micheltorena who was approaching Santa Barbara
with some four hundred men and one or two pieces of
artillery. As a result, Vicente Sánchez, the first alcalde
of Los Angeles, and Don Antonio María Lugo were
chosen. This latter was a man well esteemed by General Micheltorena and they treated each other as *com-
padres.*

The commission arrived at Santa Barbara with the
official letter from the assembly to the general, in which
was expressed the decision of that corporate body beg-

---

142 Francisco de la Guerra was active in political affairs. According to
Bancroft he took no pains to conceal his hostility to the Americans. However,
following the Mexican War, he served for several terms as mayor of Santa
Barbara beginning in 1851 during the American period. Francisco died poor
in 1878 at the age of sixty years.

143 Francisco Figueroa came to California in 1833 with his brother José and
was given the appointment of contador (auditor) of Monterey. In 1837 he
was involved in the revolt against Alvarado. In 1844-46 Francisco was a
member of the Assembly, and somewhat active against the Americans. In 1850
he served as city treasurer of Los Angeles.

144 Agustín Olvera came to California in 1834 from Mexico with the Híjar-
Padrés colony. His early life was active in political matters, for example in
1846 he was secretary of the Assembly under Governor Pío Pico. He was a
grantee of Rancho La Ciénega. At the end of the Mexican War in California,
he, together with General Andrés Pico, signed the Treaty of Cahuenga. Following the war Olvera became a lawyer, and in time served as judge and
county supervisor. Bancroft says of him, "Don Agustín was a man of good
abilities and reputation, who died in Los Angeles shortly after '74." Olvera is
perhaps best remembered for the street that bears his name at the Los Angeles
Plaza. Olvera Street is a well known tourist attraction.

ging him to refrain from marching on Santa Barbara, meanwhile the assembly would recognize him as jefe superior político. According to the report of the commissioners on their return, the general received them with great contempt, replying verbally that he was not subject to that body nor did he recognize its authority whatever. He did not reply in written form. The commissioners said Micheltorena was coming in anger, determined to make himself respected. I immediately reconvened the chamber and had the commissioners give their report.

After discussing what should be done, the assembly resolved not to recognize the authority of General Micheltorena as governor, to do so being destructive to the country – and that the senior voting member should take charge of the reins of government. By virtue of this resolution, I immediately took the oath of office before the second voting member and from that moment, I was recognized as the acting governor.

I gave orders to the first alcalde to call together the townspeople, and while they were gathered at the town hall I made a speech manifesting the reasons why it had been necessary not to recognize Señor Micheltorena as the superior political authority, and that I should be placed at the head of the political destinies of California. I asked for their cooperation in defense of their liberty and interests and they all offered it, including those born in foreign countries. Among them, I will cite the ones that figured most prominently: Don Julian Workman,[145] Don Alejandro Bell, [146] Don Santiago

---

[145] Julián Workman's given name was William, but to the Mexicans he was known as "Julián." A native of England, he came to California in 1841 by way of Taos and Santa Fe where he was a successful trader. Workman,

McKinley,[147] Don Luis Vignes, Don Juan Temple, Don Abel Stearns, and others.

Immediately after, I appointed captains to organize military companies with which to confront the enemy. The captains named were: Workman, Juan Gallardo, and Juan Crispin Pérez.[148] There were many others named by Don José Castro who was already recognized as comandante-general.

I, of course, informed Castro of the assembly's resolution and ordered him to prepare himself to go to San Buenaventura to hold there the enemy until such time

together with John Rowland, led the Workman-Rowland party of immigrants and on their arrival in southern California the two leaders purchased the Rancho La Puente. As Pico mentions, Workman was a leader in the revolt against Micheltorena. In 1868 he and Francis Pliny F. Temple established a bank in Los Angeles. However, this bank failed in 1876, and Workman in remorse committed suicide at the age of seventy-six.

146 Alejandro (Alexander) Bell came from his home in Pennsylvania to California in 1842 by way of Mexico where he had lived several years. In 1844 he married Nieves Guirado and became prominent as a trader. He took sides with Pío Pico against Micheltorena and Sutter. During the Mexican War he served as captain of the California Battalion. During the American period Bell was quite successful. In 1871 at the age of seventy he passed away. Attorney and writer Horace Bell was a nephew.

147 Santiago (James) McKinley came to California in 1824, a Scot sailor-boy of eleven who left his ship at either San Francisco or Santa Barbara. He, in time, became active on the coast as an agent for Thomas Larkin and in turn acquired a trading schooner, the "Ayacucho." In 1842 he was in partnership with Fitch and Paty. He supported Pío Pico in the movement against Micheltorena and during this period was one of the buyers of the mission estates of San Juan Capistrano and San Luis Obispo. During the Mexican War he was placed under arrest by Lieutenant Maddox with a view of extorting information about Andrés Pico's activities. McKinley married Carmen Amesti. He died in Monterey in 1875. Bancroft states: "Don Santiago was a man of good repute throughout his long career in California."

148 Juan Crispin Pérez was a part owner of Santa Gertrudis Rancho (Los Angeles County) in 1821-30, and auxiliary alcalde there in 1831-36. In 1835 he was granted Paso de Bartolo Viejo Rancho on the San Gabriel River (Los Angeles County) that was later purchased by Pío Pico.

as the government could complete its arrangements and preparations for the struggle.

Castro marched for San Buenaventura about November or December 1844, and remained there for a few days. When Micheltorena began his march from Santa Barbara, he met Castro in San Buenaventura. Castro had some one hundred fifty men, more or less, since a few had joined him in Los Angeles. There was a skirmish and Castro retreated, keeping Micheltorena's attention occupied.

By the time Castro arrived at Cahuenga, I had organized a force of about three hundred men (among them, twelve or fifteen foreigners) and two pieces of artillery, all of which I placed at Castro's command. Also at his side was Señor Juan Bautista Alvarado (ex-governor), who had also been in Los Angeles with him.

The day prior to the arrival of Micheltorena at Cahuenga, Castro notified me that the enemy was approaching. Immediately, I went to the camp of our troops and apprised myself of the means of defense that had been taken. One of them was to have established an advance of twenty-five men under the command of Captain José Antonio de la Guerra on the other side of Encino.[149]

Castro and I were in conference when news came that Micheltorena and his force were nearing Encino. At my recommendation, Castro ordered that all should march to take possession of Encino. We could not take

[149] On August 5, 1769, the expeditionary force of Gaspar de Portolá spent the night in a valley of oaks, an area fifteen miles northwest of present day downtown Los Angeles, and gave to it the name of Valley of Santa Catalina de Bononia de Los Encinos. Where Portolá was entertained by Indians there is today the community of Encino in the San Fernando Valley.

it as it was already in the hands of Micheltorena who
had arrived there before us. Our force halted and Castro, Alvarado, my brother Andrés, Don José Antonio
Carrillo, Captain Workman, I, and others went to look
for the most favorable place in which to engage the
enemy.

Castro placed the culverin [cannon] on the *Camino
Real* in the charge of Auxiliary Ensign Luis Alta-
mirano, with the artilleryman named José Ignacio
Aguilar.[150] The other piece, under Captain Francisco
Rico,[151] was placed so that in conjunction with the first,
Micheltorena would be caught between two fires.

The next day at nine o'clock a.m. hostilities commenced with an artillery duel at a considerable distance. Not one man was killed or wounded as a result
of this firing. One horse, mounted by one of Captain
Villavicencio's soldiers, perished. A man from Los Angeles had his hat blown off by a discharge of grape-shot,
knocking him off his horse.

During the shooting, I, together with Alvarado and
Ramón Malo,[152] whom I brought as secretary, went to

---

150 José Ignacio Aguilar is remembered largely because of his cannoneering
at the Battle of Domínguez, where he caused the retreat of Captain Mervine's
forces by the judicious use of the "Old Woman's Cannon" that since his become one of the legends of the Mexican War.

151 Francisco Rico was born at Monterey about 1820 and his early years
were in association with the Monterey customs house as a clerk. In the revolution against Micheltorena he was quite active. During the Mexican War he
was second-in-command under General Flores, but later led a sub-revolt
against Flores when it was feared Flores was going to abscond to Mexico
with the state treasury. Following the war he was a supervisor of a rancho in
Monterey County. In 1877 he gave his "Memoris" to Bancroft which was
mainly his personal observation of the war years. Thomas Larkin describes
Rico as "an honorable, straightforward man of good standing, but with little
property."

152 José Ramón Malo is mentioned in Bancroft only as being the grantee of
Purísima and Santa Rita ranchos near Santa Barbara.

the site of the culverin and afterwards to the other piece commanded by Francisco Rico. He promised he would defend the post with honor and asked me to withdraw out of danger. This I did, accompanied by the two above mentioned, and we stationed ourselves in a safer place where we proceeded to have a bite to eat. At this, there was a cannon shot very close to us and Alvarado said, "Since we are not taking part in the fight and still it came so close to us, we might as well join in the action or move to a safer spot," which we did, locating ourselves in a place situated between our two pieces.

I do not want to let pass in silence a curious occurrence about Señor Alvarado. At dawn of the next day, he came to me and asked to be permitted to fire the first cannonade to greet our opponent. On receiving my permission, he fired the first shot.

After being there some time, Don José Antonio Carrillo, who was the senior general, came and told me in the name of Castro that General Micheltorena wanted to suspend fire. I answered not to grant it and to continue firing until he surrendered his arms to the government.

After a while Carrillo returned with the same request and I gave him the same response.

Finally, he came for the third time and then I replied, "Tell the General to comply with the orders of the government." After that, still accompanied by Alvarado and Malo, I came down to where our forces were posted at the same point where the culverin was emplaced. Just then I saw that Captain Workman and Don Santiago McKinley had dropped their arms and gone toward Micheltorena's forces but they were fired upon and turned back.

I asked the commander of the culverin, Altamirano, for General Castro and he replied he had not seen him. I then went to where Workman was and told him if I again saw him attempting contact with the enemy I would not consider him a friend of mine. He protested his great loyalty, assuring me that he was incapable of betrayal.

I returned to the culverin and there found my brother, Don Andrés, who was also an aide to Commander-General Castro. I asked him for Castro but he, too, could give me no word of him. I walked a short distance and in a few minutes bumped into Castro who appeared to be hiding behind a small hill near the culverin. He was wrapped in a serape, and instead of his hat, he had another made of straw such as is made by the Indians. Indignant at his behavior, I told him, "You are not a General, nor are you anything. You are just a vaquero." He replied that I should not worry and I responded that this was the time to exhibit his uniform and not to be masquerading. The two of us were alone as Alvarado and Malo had stayed at some distance.

I also asked him the reason for not keeping up the fire against Micheltorena. Upon asking him this, I saw that General Micheltorena was making a move to withdraw and then I told Castro, "Aha! See the results of not having complied with my instructions." He repeated to me that I should not worry.

In their eagerness to pursue the general, our forces became somewhat disorganized. He, Micheltorena, went in the direction of San Fernando and I assumed that he would take the road to Los Angeles by way of Cahuenga. The Santa Barbara Company commanded by Captain José Carrillo[153] (son of Don Carlos Antonio), who were near the culverin, were the only ones to maintain their post and remain in good order. I ordered them to follow me so as to occupy the house of the Cahuenga Ranch. We started on the road at double march and succeeded in reaching the house before Micheltorena, who was still about two miles distant. You must understand that Micheltorena was coming by way of the Camino Real which runs in the direction of Los Angeles. He halted when he saw us at the house.

Shortly after, Señor Castro arrived with all his forces. Micheltorena promptly changed his course towards the east in search of another road to Los Angeles. However, night overcame them and Micheltorena encamped, whereupon Castro surrounded him. This maneuver was accomplished during the night by Castro, occupying all the advantageous positions.

The following day Castro sent word that Micheltorena wished to see me to make arrangements to deliver the command to me. I went to Castro and after informing myself as to Micheltorena's wishes, I went to where he was encamped, without anyone accompanying me.

After greeting each other cordially, we retired to a point some distance from the other officers. There he offered to deliver the political command to me, adding that I should place no confidence in Castro as he would never be of any help to me, that he was telling me this as man to man and friends; that shortly war with the

---

[153] José Carrillo before being a captain in the auxiliary cavalry unit of the Santa Barbara Company, was in 1834 a master of a coastwise schooner and also a grantee of Las Pozas (Ventura County). His first wife was Catalina Ortega; his second Dolores Domínguez.

United States was going to be declared and that if I had any intentions of defending the country, I should call to my side Mariano G. Vallejo to whom, by rights, belonged the general command after his, Micheltorena's, retirement. I replied that it was not suitable to enter into an agreement of any kind with him; that Don José Castro was in charge by authority of the government of the department and he had been given instructions that I could not interfere in, deciding anything, until he should give an account of the results of his military operations. After this conversation I withdrew, returning to Los Angeles.

Very soon thereafter, Castro and Micheltorena had an understanding by which the latter promised to hand over the artillery and arms brought by Sutter's foreigners and Indians. All this was accomplished on entering Los Angeles, Don Andrés Pico receiving the artillery and all the arms at the plaza.

Micheltorena marched to San Pedro with his battalion and lodged at the home of Don José Loreto Sepúlveda.[154] He remained there several days while the ship which was to take him out of the country was being readied. He went to Monterey where he picked up his wife and several officers and the rest of his battalion that had remained there as garrison, and immediately thereafter left the port for the Republic. I did not know until after he had left the country about this circumstance of his having gone to Monterey.

I now remained recognized by all the country as governor and José Castro as comandante-general. He

<hr>

154 José Loreto Sepúlveda is listed as *juez de paz* (justice of the peace) at Los Angeles in 1842, alcalde in 1846, and grantee of Palos Colorados (Palos Verdes, Los Angeles County) in 1846.

occupied himself in organizing and managing the troops as he and Alvarado, who was colonel of the auxiliary forces, had agreed.

I never cared to mix in military matters, but I couldn't help but recognize that in reality the post of comandante-general belonged to my cousin, Don Mariano G. Vallejo, and I advised some of the officers to take the necessary steps so that he should be recognized as comandante-general. Not only was it due him for his seniority, but also because I considered him much more capable in every way; he was a man whom I could trust to carry out the policy the government had planned – to insure the peace and well-being of the country. I firmly believed that with Vallejo as the comandante-general, I would have his cooperation and help. As to Castro, I could not rely on him and his actions demonstrated how well founded my distrust was. Some of the officers recognized this, but made no effort to correct it, saying that Vallejo did not want to leave Sonoma; he feared some violent, arbitrary act from José Castro.

THE CAMPAIGN OF 1838

Before going further, I wish to recall an event that took place around 1838, during the campaign between the north and the south.

A force of one hundred fifty men had been prepared, well mounted and armed. Among them were several veteran soldiers from Baja California. The force arrived at San Luis Rey where I was administrator. It was commanded by Captain Pablo de la Portilla, Estrada,[155] Zamorano, José María Ramirez, Ignacio del Valle, and I don't recall the other officers' names.

---

[155] Nicanor Estrada came to California in 1834 as a blacksmith and political

There was a council of war and it was resolved that
I be commissioned to go to José Castro who was in Los
Angeles with his force. When the troops learned that I
was assigned to this commission, the California Company from San Diego, under the command of Captain
Estrada, was so alarmed that it was proposed for me not
to go on this mission, and it was arranged that the troops
would go first and I would follow a few hours later.
And so it was done and I overtook them halfway between San Luis Rey and San Juan Capistrano. I hur-
ried ahead and entered the latter mission about eight
o'clock that night. I was asked the password by a sentry
by the name of Pablo Véjar,[156] to which I answered,
"Mexico." He ordered me to halt and reported to his
superior. I was permitted to proceed. I asked him who
his chief was and he replied that it was Andrés Pico,
which surprised me. During the conversation Véjar informed me that Don Andrés, with two or three other
men, had declared themselves while at the Los Nietos
Ranch as in favor of those from the south; and that
Castro was in Los Angeles with his troops.

After conversing with my brother, the vanguard of
our force commanded by Señor Estrada arrived. The

exile with the Híjar-Padrés colony. Previously in Mexico he served as a captain and this rank was restored in 1835. In 1837 he aided Pío Pico and others
in the difficulty with Alvarado. Thereafter he went to Mexico as a comisionado, returning with Micheltorena in 1842 and was captain of the Monterey
Company in 1843-44. His wife was Guadalupe Díaz.

156 Pablo Véjar was born in San Diego in 1802. He joined the San Diego
Company in 1821, and later was sent to Monterey after attempting to desert.
In 1830 he was exiled to Mexico for fostering a revolt, but returned in 1833.
Again in 1837 and 1846 he was active in revolts. During the Mexican War
he was captured by Kearny's forces at the Battle of San Pasqual. In later
years, while living in great poverty at Spadra, he dictated for Bancroft the
manuscript "Recuerdos de un Viejo."

sentinel, Véjar, gave them the challenge and Estrada answered, "the Supreme Government," and ordered his troops to form in battle array ready for combat. Great was his surprise when he discovered that all the force consisted of was Don Andrés, Pablo Véjar, Brigído Morillo,[157] and Teodosio Yorba. Of course, they laughed heartily about the incident.

I went ahead with my commission, accompanied by a majordomo from San Luis Rey, Teodosio Yorba, and Brigído Morillo. Even though I warned them against the danger that should they fall into Castro's hands they would be imprisoned. But they insisted on coming with me.

At the Ranch of Los Nietos, I found the advance guard of Castro commanded by Captain Manuel Larios,[158] who notified me that he had orders to let no one pass. But at my request he sent a message to Castro notifying him of my arrival. He returned immediately with an order from Castro that Larios march to San Gabriel taking me and my companions with him. About a mile before arriving at that mission, Castro met me and, giving me a pat on the shoulder, asked me where I had been captured. I denied that I had been taken prisoner, for I had voluntarily locked up his advance guard, which Señor Larios corroborated.

Castro reprimanded him for not having disarmed my

[157] Brigído Morillo is briefly listed in Bancroft as living at San Juan Capistrano in 1846 at the age of forty-six.

[158] Manuel Larios was born at San José in 1798. He became a soldier apparently as early as 1815 and remained in the military until 1829. In Governor Alvarado's time he was an alférez of the militia. In 1839 he was a grantee of Santa Ana rancho near San Juan Bautista. He died in 1865, leaving twenty-two children from three successive wives, María A. Pacheco, Guadalupe Castro, and Rosaria Armas.

companions, and their arms were immediately taken away, among them the majordomo's lance, the same which wounded Comandante-General Victoria in 1832. That, and all the other arms, were never again seen by their owners.

We entered San Gabriel where we had a long conference relating to the instructions that I carried with me. That is, that Castro and his partisans should swear allegiance to the Constitution of Mexico, recognizing the supremacy of the general government, and in that manner we would all remain friends and recognize Señor Alvarado; otherwise, the forces would move against him and they would pursue him until he was conquered, as they had men capable of achieving this. After that conference we came to Los Angeles and again discussed extensively those same matters. But Don Pablo de la Guerra,[159] who a few days before had been in San Diego aboard a ship and had been run out of the town on suspicion of taking part with the north, told Castro that everything I had said respecting the superiority of our forces was false.

Castro chose to believe Don Pablo and did not agree to what I proposed. But at last he decided to send a

---

159 Pablo de la Guerra was born in 1819 and was by far the most prominent of the sons of José de la Guerra y Noriega. In 1838 he began his official life as customs inspector in Monterey. For several years from 1842 he was acting administrator of the Monterey customshouse. Don Pablo was said to have been in favor of an English protectorate for California. When the United States flag was raised at Monterey, he went south and a little later served as Castro's commissioner to Commodore Stockton. When Castro left California, de la Guerra returned to Monterey where he was arrested in November 1846, and kept a prisoner until February 1847. Soon after his release he went to Santa Barbara and became alcalde. After the acquisition of California by the United States he became prominent politically. He was a member of the Constitutional Convention, a state senator for several terms, acting lieutenant-governor, U.S. marshal, and lastly a judge. He died in 1874.

delegation composed of Don Anastasio Carrillo, commissioner at that time of Los Angeles, and Don Antonio María Lugo to accompany me to confer with Don Pablo de la Portilla. His instructions were to demand that Don Pablo de la Portilla withdraw his forces to San Juan Capistrano, and that Castro at that time would withdraw his to San Fernando; matters to remain so until the arrival of Governor Alvarado.

Portilla made this known to his officers and they decided to answer Castro that he should advance with his forces to the place of Lagunas[160] while the ones from the south would march until they caught sight of each other; the transactions could then take place in the field between them.

Portilla wanted me to accompany Carrillo and Lugo to Los Angeles. I went with them and having gone about two miles, I told them that I did not trust Castro, for he had promised me faithfully on his honor to release Yorba, Morillo, and my majordomo as soon as it was daylight, and he had failed to comply even though it was now twelve noon or one o'clock, and that consequently I was turning back. On parting with them Carrillo asked me what he should tell Castro. I replied that he should tell Castro that having failed in his solemn promise to me of releasing my traveling companions, I feared he would detain me too; that I had always been his friend and had done everything possible on my part to avoid dissentions between the two sections of the country, but that now if the forces should engage in battle, I would be the first to fight him.

[160] The location Pico mentions is rather vague, but possibly he refers to the Lagunas (marshy ponds) in present day Laguna Canyon, inland from Laguna Beach.

I then returned to Portilla, who was already on the road, and informed him of my decision and its cause.

Shortly after, while marching to the place designated to Castro, I saw a man coming at full gallop. I immediately recognized Don Anastasio Carrillo coming in advance of Portilla. I went to meet him. He informed me that as soon as Castro had been given the message, he burst out saying that he would not wait for the men from the south, because they were coming with too much determination. Without losing any time he beat a hasty retreat leaving behind the prisoners (whom he forgot) and several objects, among them a sabre. This was told to us afterwards by Yorba and the rest. Castro did not stop until he reached Santa Barbara. Portilla's forces stayed in San Gabriel. I believe it was about that time that Don Juan Bandini, another gentleman, and myself were commissioned to confer with Señor Alvarado – concerning the pacification of the country.

We all agreed in maintaining the peace and that Señor Alvarado should recognize the superior government of the nation and should comply with its orders. Thereupon, the forces from the south returned to San Diego but, as I said before, Señor Alvarado and his supporters failed in their promise, and the country remained in disorder. The truth is that during the time when Alvarado governed the department, there was no constitutional regime, for he acted as pleased his whim.

PICO AND THE AMERICAN INVASION

Returning to speak of my administration of government, my first acts were the naming of persons holding public posts so that the administration of justice should function properly.

I asked the assembly to determine the boundaries of my government. It was designated as far as – and including – San Fernando in Baja California.

I appointed Don Juan Bautista Alvarado administrator of the customshouse at Monterey, relieving Don Pablo de la Guerra from that post, and Don José Antonio Carrillo as minister of the supreme tribunal of justice.

I established the capital at Los Angeles as prescribed by law and the district was placed under a prefecture, reserving to myself the administration of it. I named a sub-prefect in San Diego and another in Santa Barbara. To the first place I assigned Don Ramón Argüello[161] and to the second, Don Anastasio Carrillo.

The northern part constituted the second district and at its head I placed as prefect my nephew, Don Manuel Castro y Pico,[162] with his residence at Monterey. He, in

---

[161] José Ramón Argüello is mentioned briefly by Bancroft as secretary to the prefect at Los Angeles in 1842, suplente (substitute) juez at San Diego in 1845, and sub-prefect in 1846.

[162] Manuel Castro y Pico, born in 1821, was secretary and collector at Monterey in 1839, and secretary of the prefecture in 1842-43. He was a prime-mover in the revolt against Micheltorena, taking an active part throughout 1844-45. Castro had the misfortune to be captured and the good fortune to be exchanged to serve as a comisionado to make a treaty with the defeated Mexican forces. Under Pico's new administration he was made prefect of the Monterey district, also a lieutenant in the Monterey Company. He was a valuable aid to Pío Pico in the Pico-Castro difficulty. In 1846 he was promoted to captain of the Santa Barbara Company. During the Mexican War, Castro commanded the northern division, engaged in the fighting at Natividad in present Monterey County. When Flores made his hasty flight to Mexico at the war's end, Castro accompanied him. In Mexico Don Manuel remained in the military and rose to the rank of colonel. He returned to California in 1852, and for the most part resided in San Francisco, however, he never married nor became an American citizen. Bancroft says of Don Manuel, "true to his country's cause, with no sympathy for foreign filibusters, he exerted himself,

turn, was authorized to name sub-prefects in Yerba Buena or its surroundings.

My first secretary of government was Don Juan Bandini, who filled the office for a short time. He resigned because he thought I was not acting as he and some of his friends would wish, that is, towards persons who opposed my administration. Without boasting, I can declare that I never let myself be dominated by my secretaries, nor my relatives nor friends, much less in matters of public affairs. This probably brought about the great enmity which Don José Antonio Carrillo later had toward me.

After accepting the resignation of Bandini, I named Don José María Covarrubias in his place. He was a Mexican citizen although born in France; a man of intelligence and firmness of character who deserved all my confidence. Finally, when I sent him to Mexico on a special mission, there remained temporarily in charge as secretary of government, Don José Matias Moreno,[163] who accompanied me to Sonora in 1846.

My personal secretary was the secretary of the assembly, Don Augustín Olvera.

During most of my administration I had the assembly in session.

---

for the most part in vain, to heal foolish dissensions between California chiefs and direct their force against the invaders." To Bancroft he contributed three volumes of original papers.

163 José Matías Moreno was born in Baja California in 1817, the son of an English whaler named Brown. He was educated by the frontier padres, journeyed to Alta California in 1844, and in 1846 while captain of defensores in Los Angeles, became Pío Pico's secretary. Following the Mexican War he settled on a frontier rancho in Guadalupe, and died there in 1869. For the official writings of Moreno see: "Pío Pico's Correspondence with the Mexican Government, 1846-1848," by George Tays, in *California Historical Society Quarterly*, XIII, no. 2, June 1934.

I can say that from the moment I took charge of the government I led a very hazardous life. The superior government was, of course, notified of the causes that moved the people of California to get rid of General Micheltorena and the forces he brought with him; that order was re-established, and that throughout the department the sovereignty of the general government of the Republic was recognized and its orders would be respected.

After coming to an understanding with the prelate of the missions, who told me he was authorized to take provisions to insure the welfare of the country, I appointed a commission composed of Don Andrés Pico and Don Juan Manso [164] to visit all the missions and make an inventory and evaluation of their property. My principal objective in respect to these establishments was to abolish completely the regime of missions, and to establish pueblos in their place, reserving the necessary buildings for worship and the needs of their ministers, while suitable buildings would be assigned for ayuntamientos and public schools.

The above mentioned commission accomplished its purpose, rendering an account with inventories. This being done, with the approval of the assembly I made an announcement to the public, offering to lease what remained of the establishments. This method did not achieve good results because no proposals for rental were made to the government excepting in the case of

---

[164] Juan Manso came to California in 1844 as an employee of Henry Virmond, a German merchant of Acapulco who did considerable business in California. Aside from being appointed a commissioner in 1845 by Pío Pico to form inventories of mission estates, Manso also was a lessee of Rancho San Fernando (Los Angeles County).

San Fernando. In view of this, I let it be known to the
prelate that nothing was accomplished and that it was
necessary to turn to other methods, which was to sell the
establishments. In effect, towards the end of my term in
office, I put up the missions for sale, succeeding in
getting rid of some of them for such an insignificant
amount that it makes one ashamed to mention it. But
I was determined to end the mission system at all cost,
so that the properties could be bought by private individuals, as it was set forth in the law of colonization.

During my government there came to California
Don José María Híjar, the same who came as director
of colonization in 1834, with a commission from the
superior government. I do not recall what his mission
was, but he did not interfere in the administration.

On September 13, 1845, the supreme government
honored me by appointing me governor of the department by virtue of the proposal made by the assembly in
June of that same year.

When the mail from Mexico reached my hands, the
first communication I opened was that of my being
named governor, which I concealed, keeping it in my
possession for about four months before I made it public because I did not want to be governor. On the contrary, I wanted to be free of a load that was beyond my
strength and that would be a burden to me, particularly
because of all the dissensions existing and because of
the danger of a foreign invasion which was threatening,
without resources to prevent it as was my duty.

The instructions I gave Señor Covarrubias when I
sent him to Mexico were to make known to the government the absolute lack of resources that existed in the
country to defend itself in case of a foreign invasion,

and also to ask the government to relieve me from my office, replacing me with someone considered capable of such difficult undertakings in such critical circumstances.

I requested Señor Covarrubias, moreover, that in case his efforts were not heeded by the government, he was to approach the head of the English naval forces in the Pacific, whom he would be able to contact at Mazatlán or Acapulco, and propose to him in my name that in case the general government of Mexico should be disinterested in our protection, obliging us to rebel against it, California would place itself under the protection of His Britannic Majesty.

This matter was frequently discussed in Los Angeles among most of the prominent people. Some of them favored the protection of the Americans, others of the English, still others of the French, but all were of the opinion that independence should be proclaimed and they pressed me to declare it. But I did not accede to it because it was dangerous if it was not done in agreement with the comandante-general of the northern towns. Several times I summoned José Castro, so as to reach an agreement on this matter, but he was wary of coming – for fear I intended to take him prisoner. On the other hand, it was not prudent for us of the south to take such a step without the cooperation of the north, as this would place us in a very compromising situation.

Señor Covarrubias, on his return, informed me that he had had an interview with the English admiral, who was well disposed to the project. The truth was that he came with the intention of establishing relations with the government of California, but on his arrival he found the flag of the United States already flying over the territory and, of course, he did not have an opportunity to do anything.

I have previously said that from the moment I took charge of the government, I led a troubled life. When Señor Castro retreated to Monterey, he left a considerable force here in Los Angeles under the command of José Antonio Carrillo, with the rank of major-general, quartered in the curate's house. I do not recall the reason why some civilians were imprisoned there, guarded by troops. One day I was informed that on account of the threats from the major-general and because of his despotic manner toward these prisoners, they were determined to revolt one night and take the barracks. I called Señor Carrillo and informed him of what had come to my attention so that he should take the necessary measures. One of his provisions was to tell the captain of the company, Don Ignacio Palomares,[165] to be on the alert and at the slightest movement fire on the prisoners. This was heard by the prisoners, who were very indignant. They put into effect their plan, seized the arms and an artillery piece, fired shots over Carrillo's house, and in a few moments made their escape. There were not more than six or eight prisoners, men known as of good character. The soldiers returned to the barracks when these were vacated.

The next day Captain Palomares set out in pursuit of

165 Ignacio Palomares was born February 2, 1811 in Los Angeles. In his early years he served as an officer in the Mexican Army. Together with Ricardo Véjar, he rented land west of present day Beverly Hills, and there raised cattle. On April 15, 1837, Governor Juan Bautista Alvarado granted them Rancho San José in the present Pomona-Walnut valley. Palomares was a successful rancher and a prominent leader in the community, serving several times as a judge in Los Angeles, and in 1844 was captain of the *defensores*. In 1846 he took part in a movement against Flores. His home, now known as Adobe de Palomares, is a visitor attraction in Pomona.

the prisoners but he did not capture them. One evening four or five days later a man came to tell me that the prisoners wished to have an audience with me. I went to see them at the place where they were, and they told me that the cause of the matter was the bad treatment of Señor Carrillo who, when drunk, insulted and mistreated them with cruelty; that they were willing to submit to the will of the government, so that they might be judged. I advised them to present themselves the next day to the alcalde, who was the person who should know of their grievances. This is what they did. They were judged accordingly and absolved.

Señor Carrillo continued in command of the force. I must here mention that the number of persons of standing in the country had greatly declined because of the fact that Don José Castro, on his own and without authority, appointed captains, lieutenants, and ensigns wholesale in each town he came to and these poor creatures really believed that they were enjoying the ful privileges of the military, and came to the point of attempting to disregard the civil authorities. And not without pride do I say that even though San Diego was one of the smaller, less populated towns, it was never so dominated, and was the only one that had no officer appointed by Castro, because there we recognized him as a nobody.

In a conversation I had with Castro when I was governor, I asked him for what reason he gave posts as officers to those ignorant men instead of advising them to dedicate themselves to working and supporting their families. He answered me that the major plan was that those were the men who would be put at the front when danger was imminent. He would use them as targets or spies or anything else that was convenient to his plans.

I do not recall in which manner there came to my hand some correspondence of Don José Antonio Carrillo with Captain José Antonio de la Guerra and with Captain José Carrillo (captains created by Castro), the contents of which were plans schemed against the government of the country, in accordance with Señor Castro, to oust me from my post. One of the letters set the date on which the governor was to be surprised and the government taken over. Even though I had all this information, I took no provisions until the night designated for the attack, when a soldier from Captain Felipe Lugo [166] (who was supposed to attack my home by order of José Antonio Carrillo) informed me that sixty men had been gathered under the command of Lugo to carry out the plan. I sent him back to his company to observe their movements and give me a timely account of them as well as the number of arms that the conspirators possessed.

The soldier returned a second time and told me that the plotters had several pistols and muskets and four or five hatchets to break down the doors.

He told me, besides, that they had not yet carried out their plan because Lugo was awaiting written orders from José Antonio Carrillo. Lugo had asked him two or three times to send them, and Carrillo had not yet done so.

I ordered the soldier for the second time to return to

---

166 Felipe Lugo was born about 1808. His career included regidor (city councilman) at Los Angeles during various years between 1832 and 1845, a lieutenant during 1839, and judge of the plains in 1840. After the American occupation he was justice of the peace and county supervisor, residing at La Mesa, now Vernon, an industrial suburb of Los Angeles.

his company and he refused to do so. As a matter of precaution I gave him a room and bed in which to sleep, closed the door from the outside and put the key in my pocket.

The provisions I took to preserve the government were to send the governor's secretary, Covarrubias, to ask help of Don Luis Vignes. This gentleman sent me six Frenchmen armed with muskets and carbines.

At my request Don Santiago McKinley procurred nine foreigners, also armed.

Around ten o'clock that night I sent an official communication to my brother, Don Andrés, who was at the ranch of Los Nietos, calling him as an officer of the army and authorizing him to enlist in the support of the government all the men that he could find, and set out immediately to take possession of the barracks occupied by the major-general.

Between eight and nine the next morning, my brother, with twenty-five men took the barracks, after which he placed himself at the orders of the government.

I placed the man who had given me the information in the charge of the alcalde, with orders that he proceed with an investigation of the incident. I also advised the alcalde that I should be given an account of each person involved. Don José Antonio Carrillo, Hilario and Sérbulo Varelas,[167] and Felipe Lugo were found to

[167] Cérbulo Varelas (also Sérbulo Varela) and his brother Hilario, came to Los Angeles in 1838-39. They were of dubious character, given to excessive drinking, and were not looked upon with favor by most Californians. In 1845 they, together with José Antonio Carrillo, were ringleaders in a revolt to depose Governor Pico. When the plot was discovered, Carrillo and Hilario were banished to Mexico. Sérbulo was jailed from whence he escaped, or as Pico later says "was set free." The two exiles returned to California in 1846 to join Castro in his struggle with Pico. In September of 1846 Sérbulo, still the

be accomplices. I ordered that they be apprehended.

I had my brother, Andrés, conduct the individuals to jail and put fetters on each one. Carrillo was taken to the barracks where he was manacled and from there taken to jail. The other three escaped but the two Varelas were taken at the Verdugo ranch. They had fled taking with them horses belonging to the men that had come with Andrés. The Varelas were also fettered and taken to jail.

There was no prosecution against Felipe Lugo because I considered Castro and Carrillo misled him.

The three prisoners were tried. Carrillo and Hilario Varelas were sentenced to banishment from the country, and I had Sérbulo Varelas set free.

After Carrillo was legally notified of the sentence imposed by the government, I, as brother-in-law and friend, which I had been, went to the jail to see him and manifested to him that as an individual I would help in any way I could, but as a member of the government I had to act according to the law. He refused any kind of service and answered me by saying that it would not be long before I would be occupying his place. I persisted in my offers to him, assuring him of my personal friendship, and I reminded him of another occasion when he was being banished to Mexico at the time of Señor Victoria, and I had helped him with money and

---

chronic peace disturber, led a drunken force of ruffians against Captain Gillespie's handful of soldiers in Los Angeles, and by a series of circumstances set in motion the Californio's revolt that led to the overthrow of Los Angeles and the battles of Chino, Domínguez, and San Pasqual. Strangely, Sérbulo's drunken action has never been given the significant place in history it deserves.

whatever else I could, and that I had the same feelings toward him now as I had then. He maintained his refusal and I bid him goodbye.

The day after the banishment order had been pronounced, which was also the day after my visit, Carrillo asked me, through the alcalde, if he could be permitted to remain in Los Angeles that day to effect his marriage, which was to have taken place around that time, to Señorita Francisca Sepúlveda.[168] I told the alcalde that I could not consent and that he must start at ten o'clock as ordered. At ten o'clock Carrillo and Varelas left for San Diego to take the vessel for the interior of the Republic. There they embarked and continued as far as Mazatlán.

I do not know what transpired upon their arrival in Mexico, as a result of which they were set at liberty and returned to California.

Hilario Varelas came to see me and told me that Don José Antonio Carrillo had made his way to the north.

A few days later I learned that he had rejoined Señor Castro with the rank of major-general and that he was occupied in harassing the northern towns.

One of the unreasonable acts of Castro was to permit the alcalde of the town of Branciforte [now Santa Cruz] to whip the so-called Captain Francisco Sán-

[168] Francisca Sepúlveda's proposed marriage requires certain background information. As previously mentioned, Carrillo had married Pico's two sisters – Estefana in 1823 (later she died) and Jacinta in 1842 (presumably she died). In 1844 Carrilo is listed as widower. Not known is the date of marriage. Francisca was born in Los Angeles, April 11, 1826, to José Antonio Sepulveda and María Francisca Avila. In 1854 Francisca divorced Carrillo, then married James Thompson, June 10, 1869.

chez.[169] Reports of this action reached me and I brought
the matter before the assembly, whereupon it was resolved at my request to permit me to leave the capital,
to go and correct these irregularities.

Things had come to such a point that I was convinced that Castro and I could not exist at the same time
in the department and that one or the other had to go.
I gathered a force of one hundred fifty men and started
towards the north. A short distance from San Luis
Obispo I received an official note from the comandante-
general advising me of the capture of the country by
the North Americans – that is, the taking of Monterey
by Commodore Sloat. Until then I had not been notified
of the doings of Fremont nor of the happenings at
Sonoma. Having no confidence in anything that came
from Castro, I sent a messenger, Sérbulo Varelas, with
a letter to the French consul at Monterey asking him
for information as to the truth of the matter. I learned
that my messenger was taken prisoner at the consul's
house and that the latter had also been arrested by the
American authorities on suspicion of acting in accord
with the authorities of California.

I continued my march to Santa Margarita, on the
other side of San Luis Obispo. I believe the first persons from the north I encountered were Don Juan
Bautista Alvarado and Don Manuel Castro. They

---

169 Francisco Sánchez had various civil posts in both San Francisco and
San José. In 1837 he was appointed captain of the militia and at various
periods served as acting comandante at Presidio of San Francisco, including
1846 when captured by the U.S. forces. In 1846-47, provoked by the depredations of certain Americans, he attempted a revolt with the purpose of obtaining guaranties, through taking captive Alcalde Washington A. Bartlett and his
guard. Bancroft in later years takes a somewhat charitable view of Sánchez:
"he is remembered as a hospitable man, though somewhat hostile to Americans, and always regarded by them with suspicion."

briefed me on what had occurred in Monterey stating that behind them came José Castro and his forces to join the government in the defense of the country.

Shortly thereafter Castro arrived with his troops. Being all united, we embraced in token of reconciliation and all manifested great enthusiasm for the cause of our country, vowing to defend its independence and to die for it.

José Antonio Carrillo made a short speech to Castro's forces. Mine did not want to join with the others as they feared Castro was playing one of his intrigues.

Carrillo said that he was pleased because at last the principal authorities were reconciled – the ones that would be zealously occupied in defense of the country, never doubting that all would gladly cooperate towards that end.

Together we marched to Los Angeles where a few misunderstandings took place between Castro and myself and between our respective commands.

On one occasion José Castro ordered that Captain José Carrillo of the Santa Barbara Company be summoned. Carrillo refused to obey protesting that he was subject to the governor instead of the comandante-general as he was not a veteran. On hearing this, Castro made arrangements to march in person with a force of fifteen or twenty men to take the garrison of Santa Barbara. He was to be accompanied on this occasion by Manuel Castro.

Upon hearing the beat of drums for marching, I went to the door of my house and as Castro passed in front of me I called him, and the two Castros came to my house. He told me where he was going and with what intent. I cautioned him, and at last he agreed to withdraw the

soldiers on my promising that I would have José Carrillo come and explain his conduct and give satisfaction.

Shortly afterwards, I went to the house of the comandante-general to await the arrival of José Carrillo,
when I discovered that Señor Castro held prisoner
there Captain José Loreto Sepúlveda, of the auxiliary
force in the service of the government. I inquired of
Señor Castro the reason for the imprisonment and he
told me that he had been informed that there was a plot
to disavow him as comandante-general, and that he
believed even I was implicated in the plan.

My reply was, that as my forces were only auxiliary,
I had not advised them to put themselves under the
orders of the comandante-general, and that if I did
place them at his disposition, and he would be satisfied
as to my good faith, I would do so immediately, as in
effect I did, giving instructions to the captains to gather
their companies and put themselves under the orders of
the government so that I might take the necessary
measures to place them under the comandante-general.

After gathering the troops here in the public plaza,
I personally told them that the comandante-general was
the one responsible for the defense of the country, consequently they must obey his written or verbal orders.

The comandante-general took charge of the forces
and on the following day he marched to La Mesa to
prepare, according to what he told me, for the defense
of Los Angeles when the invaders should arrive.

I had news of the arrival of Fremont with a small
force at San Diego. This was, I believe, in July 1846.
According to Señor Castro, it was decided to send a
detachment to force Fremont to re-embark. It had been
agreed that the comandante-general would go in person

but he did not do so. He sent a force of some forty or fifty men commanded by Captain José María Villavicencio, but actually under Juan Bautista Alvarado who also set out with them. The force returned, I don't remember for what reason, and rejoined Señor Castro.

A few days later I received a letter from Don Juan Forster [170] notifying me that Mr. Fremont had left San Diego in the direction of Los Angeles with about eighty or ninety riflemen.

I immediately went over to the La Mesa camp to inform Castro, who on apprising himself of the contents of that letter agreed to go himself to meet Fremont. This must have been between ten and eleven a.m. I returned to the government house and spent the day packing the archives. About seven p.m. I found in the office of the secretary of government an official communication in which Señor Castro said for lack of sufficient forces and materiel of war, he was going to leave the country to give an account to the supreme government, and he advised me to do the same. Without losing a moment I convoked the deputies and that

---

[170] (Juan) John Forster, a native of England, emigrated permanently to California in 1836 after several years of trading activities between Mexico and California. In 1837 he married Isidora Pico, Pío's sister, and became captain of the post of San Pedro. In 1844 he purchased the mission lands of San Juan Capistrano, and lived there for some twenty years. During the American occupation in 1846 he was at odds with Fremont, and aided Governor Pío Pico to escape to Mexico; however, in 1847 he was most helpful in Stockton's campaign. In 1864, he bought the Rancho Santa Margarita from Pío Pico and lived out his years there, dying in 1884 at the age of seventy. Bancroft says, "Don Juan was a man who was liked and respected by all who knew him . . . a genial ranchero, famous for his hospitalities of his Santa Margarita ranch home. He was for many years a man of immense wealth; formed several plans for colonization on a grand scale, which were never carried out; but was harassed in the later years by litigation and other troubles; and the estate was sold after his death."

same night about nine or ten o'clock we were in session. I presented Castro's note and asked the chamber, in view of the comandante-general having failed us, to authorize me to take command of the forces and fight Fremont. The deputies were emphatically opposed, alleging that it was in no manner suitable for the governor to expose his person to the risk of being taken prisoner, as in that event the territory's struggle would become more difficult. They observed, in addition, that the majority of our forces were civilians – rural people – and to expose them to the dangers of war was to place their families in tribulation and misfortune.

I insisted upon the necessity of doing something and I begged the assembly to advise what measures to adopt. The assembly resolved that I should leave the country, dismissing the officials of the department so that there would be no one in authority to negotiate with the enemy.

Two incidents concerning the alcaldes of Los Angeles which I failed to relate have just come to my mind. One of them was that while José María Avila was alcalde and I was twenty years old, I came from San Diego to bring my mother here to Los Angeles. The alcalde ordered that the neighbors render their customary help at the main irrigation ditch which supplied the town with water. One of the constables came to the house of Don José Antonio Carrillo where we were lodged and told me, in the name of the alcalde, that I should go to the main outlet and work at getting the water out. I replied that I was not one of the local townspeople and that I had just arrived with my mother, consequently I was not obligated to do that hard labor. He came a second time and repeated the order of the alcalde, that I must do that work or send a substitute. Don Anastasio Carrillo was present and he offered to send someone in my place but I did not accept his offer.

It should be understood that Alcalde Avila did not know how to read nor write and ruled only by machete.

I replied that I was returning immediately to San Diego and to let the alcalde know this. I saddled my horse and got my arms ready to start on my journey. I went to where the alcalde was, greeted him, and asked if there was anything I could do for him in San Diego. He answered that what I could do for him was to dismount and go to work at the water ditch. I refused telling him that it was important I return to my town. The alcalde drew out his sabre and I took out my shot gun and prepared to prevent him from using his weapon on me. At this, the second in command who was Don Antonio María Lugo came and pleaded with me to return my gun to its place. I answered that I would as soon as I had left. I told them goodbye and left for San Diego, not returning to Los Angeles until Avila had concluded his term as alcalde.

On arriving at Santa Ana, on that same trip when I came to Los Angeles with my mother, Teodosio Yorba asked me if I carried a passport as the alcalde permitted no one to enter Los Angeles without that requisite. Right then and there I took paper and pen and forged a passport to which, at the bottom, I signed the name of the commander of San Diego, Captain Francisco María Ruiz. This I did because I knew Alcalde Avila would not discover it as he did not know how to read nor write.

The day I arrived in Los Angeles and went to present myself before the alcalde, I found him in front of the parish house having a fight with Juan Higuera,[171] a discharged soldier from San Diego. The alcalde had drawn his sabre and the man had darted forward and grabbed him by his hair. It was at this point that I drew near. A few of the townspeople came to the assistance of the alcalde. They took Higuera to jail and I had to wait there until the quarrel was over.

Avila was bald and, moreover, it was the custom to cover the head with a black kerchief. When Avila concluded tying his kerchief, I dismounted, greeting him and giving him my passport. He took it and made as if he were reading it, turning it around and at times it appeared as if he were reading it upside-down. He appeared satisfied and returned the document to me.

In 1833 I was working at the San José ranch, which belonged to the San Gabriel Mission, slaughtering cattle, share and share alike with the mission. My contract with the fathers had no limit. I could slaughter as many as I wanted as long as I gave them half the skins. I brought ten cowboys and thirty Indians on foot from the missions of San Luis Rey and San Diego, with over three hundred horses.

First I slaughtered at the ranch of Los Coyotes. There I killed twenty-five hundred head of cattle. Then I went to San José and slaughtered more or less the same number.

One day I came to Los Angeles to get provisions for

---

171 Juan Higuera. It is not certain, but this man may be the Juan José Higuera that Bancroft shows to be a landholder in Los Angeles area in 1819. Also, Bancroft reveals a Juan José Higuera released from Los Angeles jail in 1827.

my people, and while on the return trip to my camp one of Alcalde Don José Antonio Carrillo's constables caught up with me and suggested I stand guard as the other townspeople did. I refused, maintaining that I was not a resident of that area. The constable returned to the alcalde with my message and shortly thereafter overtook me a second time, giving me an order from the judge that I should appear immediately before him. I obeyed and went to court. The alcalde (who was my brother-in-law) told me I was in such a position that I must obey the constable's orders to be on duty to stand guard for which I had been called. I refused, repeating I had no obligation as I was not a resident of Los Angeles, and he sent me to jail, where I was held until the next day when he set me free, but he made me pay a fine of twelve dollars for having disobeyed his orders.

The slaughtering of cattle was done by contract and was generally practiced throughout the missions of the south, for the reason that it had come to the attention of the fathers that the government was planning the secularization of the missions. At some of these southern missions they not only killed cattle in enormous quantities, they also destroyed the vineyards which before had been cultivated with great care.

When Manuel Victoria left California, he was accompanied by the father minister of San Luis Rey, Father Antonio Peyri. He had in his service as a countryman and person of confidence, an honorary deputy named Juan Mariner,[172] a Catalonian, formerly

---

[172] Juan Mariner. Bancroft lists his name as Marine, yet admits to the other spelling. He came to California in 1795 as a Spanish artilleryman, and retired in 1821 at San Gabriel at age sixty, with rank of "lieutenant de premio" (apparently equal to "brevet" commission).

an artillery soldier at San Diego. After Victoria and
Peyri had left I had a conversation with Mariner and
he informed me that Father Peyri carried with him
thirty-two barrels apparently filled with olives, but the
majority of them were filled with bran, gold pieces
[*onzas de oro*] and silver dollars – that he, Mariner,
had packed the money with his own hands and that
most of it was in gold. Mariner was a very honorable
man of fine reputation, consequently I could do nothing
less than believe what he told me.

In the last years of the Spanish government, the
missions almost exclusively furnished the resources for
the maintenance of the troops. But this did not prevent
the officers and soldiers alike from lacking apparel and
certain necessities of life such as blankets, shoes, etc.

I personally saw, at the presidio of San Diego in the
Rancho Nacional, four soldiers going to bed in a big
tub made of skins, covering themselves with dry hay
because they had absolutely nothing else with which to
protect themselves from the cold.

PICO'S RETREAT TO MEXICO AND RETURN

In view of the disposition of the assembly, I prepared for my trip without seeing Don José Castro nor
any of his associates.

On the 13th day of August I started on my journey to
Sonora, accompanied by Don Ignacio del Valle and a
soldier of the militia named Secundino Higuera.[173] I
left about ten or eleven o'clock at night. We arrived at
the ranch of Teodosio Yorba called Santa Ana. Fremont was encamped with his forces at the home of José

---

173 Secundino Higuera. The only mention Bancroft makes is that he came to
Los Angeles in 1846.

Antonio Yorba at a distance of about one and a half
leagues from the house of Teodosio, his brother. The
next day I continued to San Juan Capistrano arriving
there at sunset or shortly after. Don Ignacio del Valle,
if I remember rightly, returned from Santa Ana to Los
Angeles. I remained hidden at San Juan for about eight
days. While I was secluded in my room, Don Juan
Bandini passed by, accompanied by Captain Santiago
E. Argüello (son of the old Captain Santiago Argüello).[174] They were lodged at the home of Don Juan
Forster where I was also hidden. Forster and the two
other gentlemen used to walk along the corridor in
front of my room. Argüello and Bandini would ask
Forster where I was as they wished to contact me and
pursuade me not to leave the country and abandon my
family (that is, my wife, my mother, and my two unmarried sisters). All this I could hear from my room.
I must mention that Bandini and Argüello were in
alliance with the American forces.

Before returning to Los Angeles the next day, they
offered to Forster to procure a safe-conduct from Fremont so that neither I nor my retinue would be molested. This they accomplished and Forster showed me
the safe-conduct signed by Fremont. (I do not know
positively in whose possession this document now is,
but I suppose that the widow of my secretary, José
Matías Moreno, must have it.)

174 Santiago E. Argüello, born about 1813, held his first public office as
receptor (collector of the port) of San Diego. In 1836-37 he took part in the
southern revolt against Alvarado. In the following years he held various public offices, as well as being a land owner of San Juan Capistrano ex-mission
lands. In 1846 he aided the Americans by serving as a captain in Stockton's
forces. He died at Maligo in 1857. One daughter married A. B. Wilcox, another William B. Coutts.

I did not consider myself authorized to accept such arrangements and I therefore retired to a camp in the mountains about two leagues from the house. There I stayed several days, having made arrangements with a neighbor to bring me provisions. Afterwards I went near my ranch of Santa Margarita, where I took the precaution of rounding up about forty or fifty mules and twenty-five or thirty horses which were in the care of three servants – Benigno Contreras, Ramón Adarga, and the third was known by the nickname of The Friar and was a native of Sonora.

One day at sunset I felt the urge to return to San Juan Capistrano to the house of Juan Forster to see my sister, who was his wife, and obtain news from Los Angeles. Benigno Contereras accompanied me. The following day Ramón Adarga came to see me at San Juan to tell me that Captain Santiago Emilio Argüello, with a force of twenty-five Americans had taken all the horses I had gathered for my trip to Sonora. That very night I returned to where I had left my horses, picked up camp and went to my house at Santa Margarita ranch. I remained hidden there for several days trying to gather horses to effect my departure from California.

Matías Moreno, the secretary, remained in San Diego in accordance with our plans, ready to start our march for the frontier of Baja California. The 7th of October I left Santa Margarita and he did the same from San Diego, meeting at a place called San Jorge about three or four p.m. of the same day. My nephew, Alejandro Carrillo,[175] also joined me. Together we fol-

---

175 Alejandro Carrillo was apparently a son of José Antonio Ezequiel Carrillo. However, Bancroft mentions only a daughter and states further, "I know nothing of any other children."

lowed the road to Baja California. The reason for taking this route was that the departmental assembly and
some of the more important people of Los Angeles
counseled me not to try to contact Comandante-General
Castro. They remarked that he, fearing I would inform
the supreme government, might attempt to endanger
my life.

On arriving at San Vicente we were joined by Ensign Macedonio González. In about two or three days
we continued on our way as my sister, Mrs. Forster,
sent word by an Indian who came by boat, that Santiago
E. Argüello had set out with a force in my pursuit.

A few days before my departure for the border, this
same Argüello had been in San Vicente with twenty-
five or thirty Americans and had forced the inhabitants
to declare themselves for the United States. On my arrival, I found the Flag of the United States flying at
the door of the courthouse. I went to the alcalde and
asked him if the frontier of Baja California had put
itself under the domination of the United States, to
which he answered that Argüello had come with a
force and the men had been unable to make any resistance. I asked him if he recognized me as the Mexican
governor and reprimanded him for having failed to
defend the sovereignty of the Mexican Republic. At
least with words, the man, with tears running down his
cheeks, asked that I forgive the fault he had committed
and said that he recognized me as governor. His name
was Ignacio Arce and he was a sergeant in the frontier
company of Baja California.

He invited me to sit down and rest. I replied I would
rest only when I should see flying the banner of our
Mexican Republic. He immediately called one of his

men and had the flag of the United States lowered and the one of Mexico put up. Then I dismounted and rested a while in the courthouse. From there I went to a lodging the alcalde had prepared for me.

After receiving the information my sister sent me, I continued my journey to Mulegé,[176] from where I embarked for Guaymas in the month of November, leaving behind Alejandro Carrillo and Benigno Contreras. (These two participated in the defense of La Paz when it was attacked by the forces.)

On the voyage to Guaymas,[177] toward morning we sighted a war vessel in the distance. In order to avoid discovery should the ship be searched, Señor Moreno and Higuera disguised themselves as sailors and I lay in bed pretending to be gravely ill.

Being thus prepared, it occurred to me that our names would appear on the ship's log as passengers. I sent Moreno to inquire of the captain if this were true. The document did show that on board ship were the governor of Alta California, his secretary, and his servant. On learning this, all thought of disguise was abandoned and I begged the captain of the schooner to put me ashore. The captain made clear the impracticability and danger involved. At last, at the risk of everything, he put us ashore in a place called Tetas de Cabra about eleven or twelve o'clock a.m. The captain gave us a guide to conduct us to Guaymas. After much toil, we arrived there about eleven o'clock p.m. I was lodged in the home of Comandante-General Campu-

---

176 Mulegé, a mission site, was founded by the Jesuits in 1705. During the Mexican war it was occupied by American troops for one day.

177 Guaymas, a principal seaport on the coast of Sonora, founded in 1760, was attacked by U.S. Naval forces in 1847 (following the war in California). After its capture, it was occupied until 1848.

zano.[178] There I met various important gentlemen of Sonora and after drinking a cup of tea they invited me to play monte in a gaming house. That night they won six hundred dollars from me.

I asked a local individual – a money lender named Don Ramón Oseguera – what the custom was there, and he informed me that it was for each to borrow what he needed, the sum to be returned the next day before starting to play. The next morning I sent him the six hundred dollars by my man-servant and that night I returned to the place with four hundred dollars in my pocket. Just as I sat down Oseguera asked me if I needed money. I replied that perhaps later if I lost what I had brought with me.

We began to play. I dealt three games of *dobladilla*[179] and bankrupted everyone for I won everything they had, about two thousand dollars.

The next night I returned to play cards and they would not permit me to bet more than fifty dollars at a time, at which I refused to play that night. Several times afterwards I played cards with the same group and I was always lucky. The last time I played with them was on the island of Ardilla where I not only won all the money they carried, but I also extended credit to each one for two hundred dollars, which they repaid within the next few days.

I remained in Sonora while maintaining relations with the supreme government of Mexico to which I

---

[178] Campuzano (no given names known) featured as the defender of Guaymas on October 16, 1847, when the U.S. frigate "Congress" and U.S. sloop "Portsmouth" and brig "Argo" bombarded the town, resulting in its surrender within the hour.

[179] A gambling game, now called Viejos, played with Spanish deck and forty cards, which is minus 8's, 9's, and 10's.

had given an account of the situation in California at my leaving, effecting this through my secretary, Señor Moreno. I requested help to return to California, or that the government dictate the steps by which the country could be extricated from the hands of the invaders. But all was in vain. Neither the general government nor the government of Sonora aided me, not even with the means to support myself there.

When the armistice between the belligerents was signed in Mexico, I took the opportunity to return to California.

In Guaymas I encountered an American frigate of war. One day the officers of that ship invited me to play "21" and I had such good luck that I won seven thousand dollars but they paid me only a small amount — about nine hundred dollars. When they failed to pay, I went to their commander and he sent word via the paymaster that his officers did not have any resources but on behalf of one of the officers the paymaster brought me a promissory note, and the nine hundred dollars were sent to me by another.

With that amount, and six hundred dollars more that was loaned to me by Dr. Kid at Hermosillo, I started out for Baja California and Los Angeles.

It has come to my attention that it was rumored that in the last days of my command in California I had sold the missions, receiving twenty thousand dollars or more for them, which I had taken with me when I left the country. I would greatly desire those who have spoken thus to present their proof and to bring to me the persons to whom the missions were sold, and for those persons to certify the amount they gave me.

The only missions I sold were: San Gabriel, San

Luis Rey, San Fernando, San Diego, San Juan Capistrano, and San Buenaventura.

The sale of San Gabriel did not become effective. That of San Luis Rey had the same fate. San Fernando was transferred to Don Eulogio de Célis as mortgage security for an amount he had made available for the needs of the government.

San Diego was given to Captain Santiago Argüello in payment of his services as his salary was owing for many years.

San Juan Capistrano was sold to Don McKinley at an insignificant sum to aid in the affairs of the government some time before my departure from here.

San Buenaventura was sold to Don José Arnaz,[180] who is still living and can testify to what he gave for it, the amount being nothing more than nominal.

Some gave money or goods to Comandante-General Castro, but at no time did they give the amount that appears in the deeds of sale. I can swear to the fact that not one single dollar came to my hands from the sale of the missions.

When I left the country the government owed me all my salaries as governor, all that was due me as deputy since 1828, besides the articles that were needed by the offices during my governorship and which were acquired from merchants solely on my personal guarantee and which debts I paid from my own funds to Abel Stearns and to Don Juan Temple on my return from Sonora.

Although I did not have thousands of dollars on

---

[180] José Arnáz came to California in 1841 as Spanish supercargo of the "Clara" in Virmond's employ. In 1844 he opened a store in Los Angeles, and thereafter acquired considerable property. His manuscript "Recuerdos" reflects much on the life and customs of the traders and rancheros of his time.

hand, I never lacked for money. My reputation and
credit were good and on my word alone I could obtain
anything I wished. That is why when the time came
that I was to leave the country, I did not have to rely
on public funds to cover the expense of my trip. In
Sonora I did not need the help of the general government of Mexico, nor of that state, and if I did ask of
Governor Gandara, it was because I considered myself
with the same rights to be helped as any other employee
of the general government, for I was owed all my back
pay without counting what was presently owed. A well
known local person once asked me if I knew why I had
been refused help by the government of Sonora. I replied that I assumed it was because the state was short
of funds. Then he told me, "The reason is, because you
are of the opposite party to Gandara, who says you have
always been a Federalist." I admitted that I had always
belonged to that party and that I would die of hunger
in Sonora rather than abandon my principles.

If I remember right, I arrived in California at my
ranch of Santa Margarita on the 9th of June 1848.
From there I went to Los Angeles, stopping one day at
the La Puente ranch of Señor Workman. Next day at
dusk I left for Los Angeles and in San Gabriel learned
that a force of Americans had left for La Puente in
search of me. I thought it prudent to send Mr. Hugo
Reid [181] to approach Colonel Stevenson,[182] who was in

---

181 Hugo Reid was a cultured Scotsman, born in the British Isles. After
spending six years in Mexico, he came to California in 1834 at the age of
twenty-three, settled in Los Angeles; and in 1835 he was accused of complicity in the Apalategui revolt. Naturalized in 1839, he was granted the Santa
Anita Rancho (Los Angeles County) by Governor Alvarado in 1841. He
married the Indian, Victoria, who had received a grant of the Cuati Rancho
(Los Angeles County). In 1849 he was a member of the convention drafting

charge of the southern district, to tell him I had returned to California – not with hostile intentions, but by virtue of the armistice agreed upon in Mexico, between the supreme chiefs of the belligerents, asking him to do me the favor of recalling the armed forces as I would present myself to him. And so the next day I went to Los Angeles and presented myself before Colonel Stevenson. This gentleman received me courteously, permitting me to withdraw to San Fernando to start official negotiations by correspondence.

I summoned my secretary of government in preference to Don José María Covarrubias, who was in Santa Barbara. As soon as he arrived at San Fernando, I entered into correspondence with the military commander of the south and also sent another communication to the governor, who was Colonel Mason.[183] From the latter I received no reply. Señor Stevenson permit-

the constitution of California. He devoted his leisure hours to studying the Indians of California, and wrote of his findings in a series of articles that appeared in the *Los Angeles Star*. He was a close friend of Pío Pico, and in 1852 verified to the U.S. Land Commission that Pico was the rightful owner of Rancho Paso de Bartolo (Los Angeles County). Hugo's death occurred in 1852. The Hugo Reid *casa* is presently an historical attraction at the Los Angeles County Arboretum in Arcadia.

[182] Jonathan D. Stevenson came to California in 1847 as colonel of a regiment of New York volunteers. At war's end, he was military commandant of the southern district. After 1848 he settled in San Francisco and involved himself in real estate ventures. In 1872 he was appointed U.S. shipping commissioner at San Francisco. Bancroft states he was, "a man of much energy, of strong will, and good executive ability, a strict disciplinarian, who performed the duties of his position in a very creditable manner."

[183] Richard B. Mason came to California in 1847 as colonel of 1st U.S. Dragoons, and succeeded Kearny as military governor of California, holding this position until February 1849. Bancroft states, "he performed most satisfactorily the duties of a difficult position, and though by his strict discipline and apparent harshness of manner he made an unfavorable impression in some quarters and inspired bitter enmities, yet his record is that of an honest, faithful, and able soldier."

ted me to return to the ranch of Santa Margarita to
await there for the governor's reply. Before this, we
had several disagreements concerning the type of passport he was granting me. I was of the opinion that I
did not need any and I told him so; I said that all he
had a right to demand of me was my word of honor, as
an employee of the Mexican government, not to com-
mit any hostile act, and to present myself upon being
called. Later, in a communication from San Fernando,
I told him I would not move from there until he gave
me a satisfactory answer. Without doubt he must have
given it to me for I came afterwards to Los Angeles
and I returned to my ranch with a safe-conduct with
instructions that I be given the consideration due my
rank as governor.

While in Santa Margarita, an officer who spoke good
Castilian came to deliver a letter from Señor Stevenson,
ordering me to present myself in Los Angeles. The
officer advised me that we should start that same day so
as to arrive in Los Angeles on the next, as those were
the orders he had from his chief. I answered him that
when I left Los Angeles, it had been done on my word
of honor, and under those same conditions I would return and in no other way; that he should leave with his
command and I would present myself in Los Angeles.
The officer replied that the force was only an escort as
an honor due the governor. I repeated what I had said
before, adding that it was impossible for me to start
until the next day. The military force was sent back but
the officer remained. He slept at my house that night
with my assurances that the following day we would be
in Los Angeles, which we actually did, arriving together at the ranch of Los Coyotes. There, the officer

stayed and I continued ahead to present myself before Colonel Stevenson.

This gentleman had me arrested in his own home. He told me his government's orders were to hold me incommunicado, but he would take it upon himself to permit me to communicate with my friends. During my arrest I ate at the same table with the commander and in all respects he treated me with the greatest consideration, even to the extent of permitting me to go on the street with a friend, but I never took advantage of his considerations.

I remained arrested perhaps three weeks, until the news arrived that peace had been made between Mexico and the United States. Then I was set at liberty and retired to my ranch.

In February of 1849 I returned to Los Angeles, bought the ranch of Los Coyotes and since then have been a resident of this jurisdiction.

RECOLLECTIONS AND PERSONALITIES

In 1821, when I was in San José, I built a shack of stakes and hides. The roof was also covered with hides. There I placed a big box that served as a counter. I had two small glasses and a large one for drinking water. The small ones were for the sale of aguardiente. Half a small glass was worth a *real,* and full two *reales.* The sale of the small glasses did not give us much profit and in order to increase this, I had the idea of using a cattle horn. I cut about a third of it and put in a false wooden bottom. I coated the inside generously with tallow and added another bottom of tallow, besides the one it had of wood. This naturally, took up much space and diminished the quantity of aguardiente it could hold.

The old drinkers were fooled, thinking that the horn contained more than it did, and they always asked not to be served in a small glass but in the horns, and with this they cheated themselves.

The use of horns prepared thusly was general in this part of the country but not until then had it been put into practice in the north.

Even though there was no lack of aguardiente in the northern missions, this article was scarce for general use, and if anyone from the south brought some aguardiente up there it was like a treasure to those people. Particularly the aguardiente from San Fernando was appreciated above any other.

While the comandante-general and his officers (among them, Captains Portilla and Zamorano) were at the ex-mission of San Luis Rey during my administration of that establishment, there occurred an uprising of Cahuilla Indians in the San Jacinto mountains. They stole some cattle and many horses from the ranch of that name. The comandante-general appointed me to lead an expedition composed entirely of soldiers against them. The officers remained at the mission leading a life of leisure. I, who did not have the slightest obligation to go out and perform such a task, told one of the gentlemen how much I desired to go to Mexico to inform the government what kind of officers they had here.

Nevertheless, I went in pursuit of the malefactors and I had the good luck of catching up with them and taking away some of the cattle that were still alive, which I returned to the San Jacinto ranch. All the Indians managed to escape.

There was a time in this country (I believe during the governorship of Don Luis Antonio Argüello) seven Indians became notorious for their robberies and depredations in the south. They committed their crimes and roamed from San Diego to Monterey and the troops that pursued them never could catch up with them.

As they were Indians from the south, they stayed here most of the time. Their names were Agustín, Juan Antonio, Martín, Fidel, Pedro Pablo, another nicknamed "Cartucho," and I don't recall the name of the seventh. They were very astute and determined men and they were the ones who assaulted my ranch taking all my goods, as I described in another place before.

After sacking my ranch, they had assaulted San Isidro, property of my López uncles. During this assault, one of my uncle's succeeded in killing Fidel. If they had not had this good fortune, my two uncles would have perished at the hands of the Indians, but they escaped with their lives, although one of them was carried out on a stretcher half dead, and the other was seriously wounded. These malefactors kept doing as they pleased until about the end of Alvarado's administration.

After having performed several of these assaults, they made peace with the whites. During the active pursuit of them, Martín and Pedro Pablo escaped to Sonora. After a short time they returned exonerated by the general government. I do not know how they obtained those pardons.

No one bothered them any more, and most of them found employment as cooks and servants, when all of a sudden it was discovered that they were plotting against the town of San Diego. They had even planned which Señoras or Señoritas each would take to himself.

When this plot was discovered, Ensign Macedónio González, who was at the frontier, was alerted. He, without noise or display and feigning ignorance of the plot, came alone to San Diego. He seized the conspirators one by one, taking them from the houses where they were employed, and without further ado, on his own authority, shot them. These were arbitrary acts but we all breathed easier.

Corporal Osuna, majordomo of the Mission of San Diego at the time of the padres, came to the presidio, which was then commanded by Don Francisco María Ruiz. He insisted that Osuna remove his hat when he passed the commander. Osuna absolutely refused, telling him that he was no longer under his authority. The captain had him taken prisoner to the guardhouse by my brother, José Antonio Pico who was then sergeant of the company, with orders to put him in the stocks. Osuna resisted saying that they could kill him or do anything they wished, but he would not enter. My brother then went to the captain to tell him what had transpired and to receive his orders. Ruiz answered, "Well, if he does not want to enter, let him go." Osuna was freed.

Joaquín Carrillo,[184] father-in-law of General Vallejo, played the violin quite well. During the time he was a soldier, there was a dance at the home of the

---

[184] Joaquín Carrillo, a native of Lower California, was for twenty-two years a soldier, including duty in San Diego. It was his daughter Josefa who was featured in the romantic marriage of Henry D. Fitch.

commander, Captain Ruiz, who was very fond of a sonata called "Malagueña." He asked Carrillo to play it and because Carrillo took his time tuning his violin, Ruiz, who was a great despot, had him put in the stocks by his head, and he sent all the ladies to their homes. All this occurred about midnight.

Dr. William Kid came from Guaymas in 1834 in the schooner "Margarita," together with Captain Hamilton, Manuel Requeña, and James Johnson and family. Kid was a native of Boston, a very able physician and a man of excellent character. He was highly esteemed for his personal, as well as his professional merits. He never married. He returned to Sonora about the year 1836. I, Pío Pico, saw him in Hermosillo in 1848 and he loaned me six hundred dollars. Afterwards, Kid came to California and visited Los Angeles that same year. He later went to the gold fields and died near Stockton.

Once, while Antonio Machado [185] was judge in Los Angeles, he was taking the declaration of Don Abel Stearns, who was resting firmly on one foot and had the other on a chair. Every time Stearns finished a phrase, Machado would interrupt by saying, "I do not pay attention to cranes," no doubt referring to the position in which Stearns was standing, much like a crane does, on one foot. After three or four reprimands to Stearns about his manners, without Stearns taking any notice or assuming a more respectful position in front of the judge, the judge suddenly gave him a slap which threw

---

[185] Antonio Machado is mentioned briefly by Bancroft. No background information of consequence is given. He was regidor (head of town council) at Los Angeles in 1833. In 1838-39 he was acting mayor of Los Angeles.

him to the ground, telling the secretary, "Listen you, I
knock down and you take notes." Machado was a tall
and heavy-set-man, without schooling, but he possessed
natural talent and good judgement and often indulged
in humorous remarks.

Near the end of the year 1845, there came a band of
Yutah Indians. The people were very much alarmed
because they believed these Indians to be very savage
and capable of doing great harm.

Stationed in Los Angeles was Don José Antonio
Carrillo, major-general, who had at his command, an
auxiliary company of civilians from Los Angeles.
When I received notice the Yutahs were nearing San
Bernardino, I asked help of Carrillo to go and meet
them and he refused me. Then I requested the alcalde
to provide me with some men to accompany me. I left
the capital with six civilians armed with lances and
muskets. I arrived at San Gabriel and was joined by a
force of fifteen men sent by Señor Carrillo. I immediately sent them back with my thanks. At the ranch of
San José de Nogales [186] I met a New Mexican named
Moya who knew the customs and the language of the
Yutahs, and he accompanied me to the encampment of
the Indians, instructing me first as to what I should do
to enter into relations with them.

I found the Indians at a place named Yucaipa.[187]
There were about thirty men and women, all of them
well mounted and armed with rifles and arrows. Our
interpreter told them who I was and that I had come to

---

186 Rancho de Nogales, of one league in the vicinity of Pomona (Los Angeles County) was granted in 1840 to José de La Cruz.

187 Yucaipa is presently a thriving community east of Redlands.

greet them, etc. They seemed very friendly and we all marched together to the ranch of San José. They camped under some alder trees while I retired to a distance of two hundred varas and there made camp. Before leaving, I asked them at what time I could return and talk with them. They replied that I should come at sunset. At that time I appeared with my interpreter. They formed a circle and I sat next to their chief. They lighted a large pipe full of tobacco. The chief puffed two or three times then passed it to me and, in accordance with the instructions of the interpreter, I gave it a few puffs and passed it to the next one and in that manner the pipe was passed around the circle until it returned to the chief. This ceremony of peace concluded, I asked the object of their trip to California and the chief replied that they brought for sale some buffalo hides and four little Indian prisoners they had taken from their enemies along the way. Three were little girls, the oldest not more than thirteen years old. I told them that in California such traffic was not tolerated, referring, of course, to the Indian children, but for them to give them to me as a gift and I would reward them. They agreed to this and I ordered them at the same time not to go beyond that place, where they could sell their hides, and to let me know four or five days before they left so I could reciprocate their gift — that is, the four little Indians.

The next day I returned to Los Angeles and placed the Indian children in the care of respectable families so that they would raise and educate them. When the Indians advised me that they were about to leave for their own lands, I sent them a gift of mares and horses, glass beads, and other objects.

LIFE IN THE MISSIONS

The mission Indians led a communal life. The married ones had their rancherías, living from one to three families in one house, according to the relationship of the members.

In the missions there were a number of large buildings. One of these was for the unmarried young men and the other was the nunnery or the place for the young girls from fourteen or fifteen and up, while the younger girls were kept with their parents.

The young men were under the special care of the alcaldes and the females under an Indian matron, either married or widowed – an older woman to whom we gave the name of Mother Abbess.

At break of dawn, the alcaldes would let the men out, and the matron the girls. The men went immediately to receive their nourishment of *pozole* or *atole*; * sometimes it was pozole of wheat, other times atole of wheat or of corn or barley. There were large containers in a nearby special building and it was called the pozolera. There the food was prepared and distributed three times daily – this was early in the morning, then at eleven o'clock a.m. and the last one at sunset. This was the invariable custom in the southern missions.

The girls were taken to wash their faces and hands and afterwards to the pozolera to have their breakfast. From the pozolera the girls went to the spinning wheels; each one received so many pounds of wool for the days work, which they had to turn in that afternoon, well spun. At eleven o'clock a.m. the girls returned to

---

* Pozole: barley or other grain boiled with beans. Atole: gruel, usually ground corn and water.

the pozolera to eat pozole or atole. In the evening after they had turned in their share of the work, they went to have their dinner at the pozolera. Generally, they had their work completed in the afternoon because the amount distributed to them in the morning was calculated to be completed during that day. After dinner the Mother Abbess would lock the girls in their dormitories and would give the key to the Father Minister.

The men generally had their work assigned to them by the alcaldes. This work was assigned both to married and single men but the married men were given their rations weekly and the married women were the ones that came to receive the rations. All the men and women who went to work outside the mission had to eat in the pozolera.

Every fifteen days a certain amount of cattle was slaughtered to be distributed amongst the entire community – the apportionment was about twenty or twenty-five pounds for each individual. The flanks and rib steaks, being the most tasty parts of the beef, were given to the girls, who were the first to claim their rations. After the girls came the married women, then those of different occupations in the order which had been established.

In each mission there were a certain number of looms and in front of each loom was a weaver. To supply the wool there were about forty or fifty carders and the boys necessary for the various small jobs. There were one or two forges according to the size of the establishment. It is well known that some missions were more prosperous than others and for the same reason it must be assumed that some had more looms than others.

Taking San Luis Rey as a model, which had been in

my charge and was considered one of the richest in the south – it was undoubtedly the most prosperous, after San Gabriel. In San Luis there were ten looms, two forges, a carpenter shop, a large shoemaking shop, and a saddlery in which twelve journeymen and a white master-craftsman were occupied in making shoes, saddles, harnesses, and other articles made of leather or hides.

There was a soap manufactory well supplied with all the necessaries.

There were large granaries or depositories for the grains and other agricultural products of the establishment. Since we had no mills, there were about twenty-five women constantly occupied in grinding wheat or corn.

The suet and fat from the slaughtered cattle was taken to the soap manufactory to be made into soap. The ribs and loins of the cattle were not given to the Indians but were assigned for the use of the padres, guests, etc. On occasion a loin of jerked beef was given or sold to someone.

There must have been some system of teaching before I assumed charge of the establishment as there were neophytes who could read, write, assist at mass, sing, and play several instruments such as guitar, violin, flute, triangle, tambourine, drums, etc.

I followed the same regimen as the padres. The general custom was that on Sunday after mass all the Indians were gathered in the plaza of the seminary.

At each ranch there was a white majordomo. In my establishment there were even three majordomos. One of them managed the internal affairs of the ranch, receiving all its produce, harvest, and manufactures.

Another, in accord with the alcaldes, named the Indians – both men and women – assigned to each type of work. The third was in charge of general business – maintaining the police, attending to the care of the orchards. This person, however, had no jurisdiction over the others, but he did visit all the ranches daily and gave an account of all he saw, and if he noticed in others any laxness in the discharge of their duties he reported it.

The field work was from six or seven in the morning until eleven o'clock. At that time the bell was rung so the Indians would come to eat. The bell was again rung at one o'clock so that work would be resumed. Their day ended at sunset.

The agricultural work consisted of plowing the ground once or twice before planting the seed. This operation was done by a yoke of oxen in charge of a laborer, using a plow with an iron point made by the Indian blacksmiths. When there was no iron at the missions or at the ranches of the settlers, they used plows made of oak or evergreen oak, without an iron point. To sow the seed, they made the rows with the same plow except that an earthboard was added to make the rows wider.

The seed was planted by hand – three, four, or five grains of corn, the same of beans. The wheat and barley were liberally scattered on the ground and then plowed and raked without using the earthboard on the plow.

The operation of raking was done by using branches of trees sufficiently large to smooth the ground to cover the seed.

The grain was harvested when it was ready, usually from July to September, although sometimes we started to harvest in May and by August all the grain was in the granaries. The latter were made of adobe walls with roofs of tule or earth.

The harvesting was done by men, women and boys and it was all done by hand. Each worker carried his basket on his back in which he put the grain. By their side were *carretas* [carts] covered with hides in which the workers would empty their baskets as they were filled.

For husking the wheat, the seed was placed in rows and each worker beat it with a stick. After that, the women, using trays made by themselves, would shake them and in this manner the grain was separated from the straw. The same operation was performed with the other grains. They were all stored in the immense granaries with the beards of the grain, but without sacks. From there it was rationed to the neophytes.

Before there was trade with the outside, the missions produced all the material the Indians used to clothe themselves. Each Indian was given a loincloth made of coarse material, a blanket, and a jacket made something like a shirt, also a coarse cloth made by the Indians themselves. The Indian women were given material for skirts and also a blanket and a blouse. Once a year they were given a dress. The cowboys were only given shoes, leather pants, and a shirt of coarse cloth. Afterwards, it was customary to purchase from the ships many things for the Indians. Among them were unbleached muslin, flannel, and printed calico.

The missions had a storehouse which was more like a well supplied store. During the time of the padres, Indians were not given stockings nor shoes, but during my time they were given many things, and they were well fed and dressed. Some Indian women even got to possess silk shawls given at my order.

I have said before that during my administration there was only an *alcalde* [to order Indians] punished by whipping. It was never necessary from that time on to punish anyone for misdeeds which were up to me to correct. If anyone committed a transgression they were turned over to the proper authorities for judgement.

In the time of the padres the Indians were punished by whipping.

Index

Note: *Family (relationship) indications are to Pío Pico.*
Subjects grouped under a single index heading are:
Ranchos; *and* Counties of California.